Between Faith and Reason

Between Faith and Reason

Essays on Catholic Modernism

Jeffrey L. Morrow

☙PICKWICK *Publications* • Eugene, Oregon

BETWEEN FAITH AND REASON
Essays on Catholic Modernism

Copyright © 2025 Jeffrey L. Morrow. All rights reserved. Except for brief quotations in critical publications or reviews, no part of this book may be reproduced in any manner without prior written permission from the publisher. Write: Permissions, Wipf and Stock Publishers, 199 W. 8th Ave., Suite 3, Eugene, OR 97401.

Pickwick Publications
An Imprint of Wipf and Stock Publishers
199 W. 8th Ave., Suite 3
Eugene, OR 97401

www.wipfandstock.com

PAPERBACK ISBN: 979-8-3852-0999-6
HARDCOVER ISBN: 979-8-3852-1000-8
EBOOK ISBN: 979-8-3852-1001-5

Cataloguing-in-Publication data:

Names: Morrow, Jeffrey L., author.
Title: Between faith and reason : essays on Catholic modernism / Jeffrey L. Morrow.
Description: Eugene, OR: Pickwick Publications, 2025. | Includes bibliographical references and index.
Identifiers: ISBN 979-8-3852-0999-6 (paperback). | ISBN 979-8-3852-1000-8 (hardcover). | ISBN 979-8-3852-1001-5 (ebook).
Subjects: LCSH: Modernism (Christian theology)—Catholic Church. | Loisy, Alfred, 1857–1940. | Cumont, Franz, 1868–1947. | Pius X, Pope, 1835–1914.
Classification: BX1396 M67 2025 (print). | BX1396 (ebook).

VERSION NUMBER 04/04/25

This book is dedicated to all of my children,
who have brought me so much joy over the past 19 years:
Maia, Eva, Patrick, Robert, John, Nicholas, and Anna

Contents

Introduction | 1

1. The Significance of Modernism: Reflections on My First Book on Modernism and How I Came to Recognize Modernism's Continued Significance | 5
2. Modernism Broadly Understood | 27
3. Modernism and the History of Religion | 42
4. Alfred Loisy's Early Biblical Scholarship | 57
5. Loisy on the Way to Vatican II | 79

Conclusion | 93

Bibliography | 95
Subject Index | 121
Author Index | 123

Introduction

THE WORLD OF ROMAN Catholic Modernism is a topic about which few seem to know much. Within the Catholic world, most seem to have the general impression that the "Modernists" were the "bad guys"—or else, they may think of them as forgotten heroes, wrongfully persecuted. Many scholars identify Catholic Modernism as an invention of Pope St. Pius X in the very encyclical he promulgated that condemned Modernism, his 1907 *Pascendi Dominici Gregis*. The trends identified in *Pascendi*, and the unnamed individuals that were the target of the encyclical, however, date further back, at least to during the time period of Pope Leo XIII. In fact, Leo's 1893 papal encyclical, *Providentissimus Deus*, was mostly directed against Alfred Loisy (though he was never named), who also happened to be one of the main unnamed targets of Pius X's *Pascendi*.[1] Loisy would be excommunicated in 1908.

Even the very definition of what constitutes "Modernism" is contested and difficult to nail down, especially if one wishes to avoid *Pascendi*'s definition, which seemed to envision an organized network of bad actors—an organized network whose existence few, if any, would grant ever existed—and whose net was so broad as to implicate, in the minds of some anti-modernists,

---

1. See, e.g., Arnold and Vian, eds., *La Redazione*.

future popes like Benedict XV and St. John XXIII.² It is not my intention here, in this volume, to settle any of these debates. Instead, what I hope to do here is examine a few of the lesser-discussed areas of Modernist studies.

In the first chapter, I discuss the contemporary relevance of Roman Catholic Modernist studies by explaining the origin of my own engagement in this field, situating my first book-length treatment within the context of Modernist studies as well as within the context of my own work within the history of modern biblical scholarship.³ This chapter is a revision and expansion of a paper I initially presented at La Société Internationale d'Études sur Alfred Loisy in San Diego, 2019, titled, "On *Alfred Loisy and Modern Biblical Studies* (2019)."

In the second chapter, I take a look at the broader so-called modernism that was throughout Europe, with a special focus on Belgium, although not exclusively so. This chapter is an engagement with the scholarly articles published in Danny Praet and Corinne Bonnet's edited volume on this topic.⁴ This second chapter is a revision and expansion of a paper I initially presented at La Société Internationale d'Études sur Alfred Loisy in 2018 in Denver titled, "Engaging Danny Praet and Corinne Bonnet's *Science, Religion and Politics during the Modernist Crisis* (2018)." That paper was reworked and shortened into a book review that was published by *Heythrop Journal* in 2021.⁵ I owe *Heythrop Journal* thanks for letting me reuse material from that review in this expanded and revised chapter.

My third chapter looks more closely at Alfred Loisy's post-excommunication contributions to the discipline of the history of religion in France. Here I engage especially with Annelies Lannoy's work on Loisy's place within this history.⁶ This chapter is a revision

---

2. On the difficulties of defining "Modernism" see, e.g., Arnold, "Newman and '*Modernism*,'" 11–17.
3. Morrow, *Alfred Loisy*.
4. Praet and Bonnet, ed., *Science, Religion and Politics*.
5. Morrow, review of *Science, Religion and Politics*, 130–32.
6. Lannoy, *Alfred Loisy*.

INTRODUCTION

and expansion of a paper I initially presented at La Société Internationale d'Études sur Alfred Loisy in San Antonio in 2021 titled, "Response to Annelies Lannoy's *Alfred Loisy and the Making of History of Religions*." That paper was reworked and shortened into a book review that was published by *Theological Studies* in 2022.[7] I owe *Theological Studies* thanks for allowing me to reuse material from that review in this expanded and revised chapter.

My fourth chapter explores Alfred Loisy's work in biblical studies in more depth. I take a look, not only at his work that was prior to his 1908 excommunication, but even earlier, prior to his 1893 forced removal from teaching at the Institut catholique. Much of this material constitutes the reason for his dismissal, triggered Pope Leo XIII's *Providentissimus Deus*, and contributed to Loisy's eventual excommunication from the Catholic Church in 1908. This chapter originated as an article published in the scholarly journal *Modernism* in 2018.[8] I owe *Modernism* thanks for permitting me to reuse material from that article in this revised version here in this chapter.

My fifth and final chapter takes a look at an underexplored way in which some of Loisy's thoughts in ecclesiology, in his discussion of the nature of the church, anticipated some of what came in the Second Vatican Council, particularly on the notion of the universal call to holiness. This chapter originated as a paper I initially presented at La Société Internationale d'Études sur Alfred Loisy in Atlanta in 2015 titled, "The Kingdom of God and the Church: A Look at Loisy's Ecclesiology in *L'Évangile et l'Église*." An expanded and heavily revised version of that paper was later published in the journal *Downside Review* in 2019.[9] I owe *Downside Review* thanks for allowing me to incorporate some of that material in this revised chapter.

I think the study of Modernism is an important field of enquiry that helps uncover important intellectual as well as political currents in the late nineteenth and early twentieth centuries

---

7. Morrow, review of *Alfred Loisy*, 160–61.
8. Morrow, "Études Bibliques," 12–32.
9. Morrow, "Thy Kingdom Come," 3–13.

that help contextualize later developments in twentieth century Catholic theology, but also in Catholic biblical scholarship. My hope is that this small volume contributes to the discussion, making some of my work that has been done in this area, accessible to a broader audience.

1

The Significance of Modernism

Reflections on My First Book on Modernism and How I Came to Recognize Modernism's Continued Significance

Introduction

SEVERAL YEARS AGO I had the opportunity to discuss my first book dealing with Modernism, *Alfred Loisy and Modern Biblical Studies*, at a session devoted to the study of Roman Catholic Modernism, at the meeting of La Société Internationale d'Études sur Alfred Loisy, which meets annually alongside the American Academy of Religion.[1] I have been privileged to have been an active participant in this scholarly forum for studies on all things pertaining to what we might call Roman Catholic Modernism. The American branch of La Société basically emerged after the American Academy of Religion "suppressed" the Roman Catholic

---

1. Morrow, *Alfred Loisy*. That particular session was held in San Diego that year, in 2019. My paper was titled, "On *Alfred Loisy and Modern Biblical Studies* (2019)."

Modernism Group in 1994.² Prior to that decision, the Roman Catholic Modernism Group, which itself emerged from the Nineteenth Century Theology Group, the American Academy of Religion's longest consecutive running unit, had been running annual sessions for eighteen years, since 1976.

We can speak of the Roman Catholic Modernism Group being "suppressed" because it had already earned the status of being a permanent group with the American Academy of Religion. The American Academy of Religion allowed the group to continue for five more years, making 1999 the last year of the Roman Catholic Modernism Group's 23-year history.³ Charles [C.J.T.] Talar, who had been a long-time member of the Roman Catholic Modernism Group, continued to facilitate the study of Roman Catholic Modernism at the American Academy of Religion through his leadership of the American branch of La Société.

A number of important book volumes emerged from the papers initially presented at the Roman Catholic Modernism Group.⁴ The work of La Société has continued this scholarly production. All of the chapters of this present volume, except for the fourth, originated as papers I presented before La Société, including this present chapter. My own book-length contribution, *Alfred Loisy and Modern Biblical Studies*, included chapters taken from two presentation originally made before La Société, and another that was initially presented at the Nineteenth Century Theology Group, a related unit within the American Academy of Religion.

What I hope to do in this initial chapter is situate my own contribution, *Alfred Loisy and Modern Biblical Studies*, within the broader context of both my own overarching scholarly work as well as that of the contemporary scholarly study of Roman Catholic

    2. I take the phrase "suppressed" from Portier, preface, ix.
    3. In addition to the few comments in Portier, preface, ix–xi, see McKeown, "After the Fall," 111–31, on the history of the Roman Catholic Modernism Group of the American Academy of Religion.
    4. These would include: Barmann and Talar, ed., *Sanctity and Secularity*; Jodock, ed., *Catholicism Contending with Modernity*; and Barmann and Hill, ed., *Personal Faith*. There are many other monographs and single articles published in journals that came from this work as well.

Modernism. My hope is that it will highlight some of the continued relevance of the study of modernism. I begin first, by explaining what led me to engage in this study that eventually turned into my first book dealing with modernism. After going over how I got into modernist studies, and Loisy in particular, I then summarize my book's main arguments. Finally, in the concluding portion of this chapter I suggest some ways my work contributes to our understanding of Roman Catholic modernism.

My Entry into the History of Modern Biblical Criticism

My interest in the study of Roman Catholic Modernism came from my time as a doctoral student studying under William Portier at the University of Dayton; in addition to serving as my dissertation director, Portier taught four of my doctoral seminars. I had been drawn to the study of the history of biblical interpretation, particularly in the modern period. Part of this interest was sparked by a disparity in my own academic formation up to that time. Growing up as an agnostic in a Jewish home I assumed a mostly skeptical position toward the Bible.[5] At Miami University, in Oxford, Ohio, although I found such skeptical approaches to the Bible in many of my classes as a comparative religion major, I had become an evangelical Protestant Christian, and then through evangelicalism became Catholic and my own studies had shown me a different approach to the Bible, one confirming it as sacred Scripture.

Miami's Comparative Religion department was tied for the oldest such department at a state school in the U.S., but it was in fact the oldest that had been solely state funded.[6] Their faculty had largely been trained at the University of Chicago under scholars

---

5. My own journey from agnostic Judaism, through evangelical Protestant Christianity, to Roman Catholicism is recounted in Morrow, "Great Love Affair," 429–38; and more thoroughly in Morrow, "Reluctant Conversion," 161–92.

6. On Miami's Department of Comparative Religion see Morrow, "75 Years," 81–87.

like Mircea Eliade[7] and Joseph Kitagawa,[8] or at Harvard. The biblical studies taught in that department, was of a very high quality, but was also very representative of biblical studies in the academy more broadly speaking, which follows a procedural or methodological agnosticism, what John Milbank labels a "methodological atheism."[9] I learned a tremendous amount from the faculty in this department, but my own conversion, and that intellectual process, disposed me more to the methods of one of Miami's renowned ancient historians Edwin Yamauchi.[10]

Yamauchi was trained primarily in ancient history and ancient languages (he had studied some 20 languages). Yamauchi's main mentor had been the famous scholar of classics, the Bible, and the ancient Near East, Cyrus Gordon, who founded Brandeis University's Department of Mediterranean Studies where Yamauchi earned his PhD.[11] Yamauchi was an evangelical Protestant scholar who, although specializing in the study of Gnosticism,[12]

7. On Eliade see Ginzburg, "Mircea Eliade's Ambivalent," 307–24; Smith, "Eternal Deferral," 215–39; Idel, "Camouflaged Sacred," 159–96; Ricketts, "Mircea Eliade," xi–xiv; Ellwood, "Eliade," 1–22; Segal, "Eliade on Myth," 65–76; Allen, "Eliade's Phenomenological Approach," 85–112; Allen, *Myth and Religion*; and Ellwood, *Politics of Myth*, 79–126.

8. On Kitagawa see Miller, "Pedagogy of Religion," 117–27; and Reynolds and Ludwig, "Joseph Mitsuo Kitagawa," 1–10.

9. Milbank, *Theology and Social Theory*, 253.

10. On Yamauchi see Yamauchi, *Asian American*; Morrow, "Yamauchi," 2549–50; Morrow, "Edwin M. Yamauchi," 653–54; Maier, foreword, xi–xiv; Wineland, preface, xv–xvii; Calvert, "Edwin M. Yamauchi," 1–23; and Yamauchi, "Ancient Historian's View," 192–99.

11. On Gordon see especially, Rendsburg, "Cyrus H. Gordon," 137–43; Gordon, *Scholar's Odyssey*; Lubetski and Gottlieb, "Forever Gordon," 2–12; Feldman, "Homer," 13–21; Marblestone, "Mediterranean Synthesis," 22–30; Morrison, "Continuing Adventure," 31–35; Rendsburg, "Someone Will Succeed," 36–43; Tsumura, "Father of Ugaritic," 44–50; and Yamauchi, "Magic Bowls," 51–55.

12. See, e.g., Yamauchi, "Elchasaites," 49–60; Yamauchi, "Mandaic Incantations," 253–68; Yamauchi, "Issue of Pre-Christian," 72–88; Yamauchi, "Gnosticism and Early Christianity," 29–61; Yamauchi, "Jewish Gnosticism," 467–97; Yamauchi, "Descent of Ishtar," 140–71; Yamauchi, "Pre-Christian Gnosticism," 129–41; Yamauchi, "Apocalypse of Adam," 537–63; Yamauchi, "Mandaeism,"

THE SIGNIFICANCE OF MODERNISM

was also known especially for his work on ancient Persia,[13] Ezra,[14] Esther,[15] Nehemiah,[16] and Daniel,[17] as well as biblical archaeology more broadly.[18] His work, especially on the historical Jesus, was very influential for me.[19] Meeting with Yamauchi during his

---

563; Yamauchi, "Some Alleged Evidence," 46–70; Yamauchi, *Pre-Christian Gnosticism*; Yamauchi, "Gnostics and History," 29–40; Yamauchi, *Gnostic Ethics*; Yamauchi, "Mandaic Magic Bowl," 49–63; Yamauchi, *Mandaic*; Yamauchi, "Present Status," 88–96; and Yamauchi, "Aramaic Magic Bowls," 511–23.

13. See, e.g., Yamauchi, "Reconstruction," 350–74; Yamauchi, "Did Persian," 282–97; Yamauchi, "God and the Shah," 80–99; Yamauchi, "Persians," 107–24; Yamauchi, "Ahasuerus," 105; Yamauchi, *Persia*; Yamauchi, "Religions," 123–29; Yamauchi, "Susa," 426–30; Yamauchi, "Achaemenid," 5–81; and Yamauchi, "Darius," 425.

14. See, e.g., Yamauchi, "Ezra," 394–467; Yamauchi, "Post-Biblical Traditions," 167–76; Yamauchi, "Reverse Order," 7–13; and Yamauchi, "Archaeological Background of Ezra," 195–211.

15. See, e.g., Yamauchi, "Vashti," 825–28; Yamauchi, "Mordecai," 272–75; Yamauchi, "Notes," 670–730; and Yamauchi, "Archaeological Background of Esther," 99–117.

16. See, e.g., Yamauchi, "Model Leader," 266–76; Yamauchi, "Nehemiah," 171–80; Yamauchi, "Archaeological Background of Nehemiah," 291–309; Yamauchi, "Was Nehemiah," 132–42; and Yamauchi, "Two Reformers," 269–92.

17. See, e.g., Yamauchi, "Archaeological Background of Daniel," 160–70; Yamauchi, "Daniel," 37–47; Yamauchi, "Hermeneutical Issues," 13–21; and Yamauchi, "Greek Words," 170–200.

18. See, e.g., Yamauchi, "Current Status," 1–36; Yamauchi, "Archaeology and the Bible," 46–54; Yamauchi, "Archaeology of Biblical Africa," 6–18; Yamauchi, "Archaeology and the Gospels," 1–12; Yamauchi, "Obelisks and Pyramids," 111–15; Yamauchi, "Scythians," 90–99; Yamauchi, "Ramsay's Views," 27–40; Yamauchi, *Foes from the Northern*; Yamauchi, *Scriptures and Archaeology*; Yamauchi, *Archaeology of New Testament*; Wiseman and Yamauchi, *Archaeology and the Bible*; Yamauchi, "Recent Archaeological Work," 37–116; Yamauchi, "Documents from Old Testament," 1–32; Yamauchi, "Decade and a Half," 710–26; Yamauchi, "Archaeological Confirmation," 54–70; Yamauchi, *Stones and the Scriptures*; Yamauchi, *Greece and Babylon*; and Yamauchi, *Composition and Corroboration*.

19. His work relating to the historical Jesus and related studies includes: Yamauchi, "Did Christianity," 149–56; Yamauchi, "Life, Death, and the Afterlife," 21–50; Yamauchi, "Jesus Outside the New Testament," 207–29; Yamauchi, "Archaeology and the Gospels," 1–12; Yamauchi, "Episode of the Magi," 15–39; Yamauchi, "Archaeology and the New Testament," 645–69; Yamauchi, "Easter," 4–7, 12–14, and 16; Yamauchi, "Historical Notes on the (In)comparable,"

office hours and taking an ancient history undergraduate seminar from him instilled in me a great appreciation for evangelical biblical scholarship, particularly in regard to the history of the Old Testament. I thus devoured works by scholars like the Egyptologists James Hoffmeier[20] and Kenneth Kitchen[21] as well as Assyriologists and Archaeologists like Donald Wiseman[22] and Alan Millard.[23]

7–11; and Yamauchi, "Historical Notes on the Trial," 6–11.

20. Hoffmeier's important works include: Hoffmeier and Rendsburg, "Pithom and Rameses," 1–19; Hoffmeier, "Egyptian Religious Influences," 3–36; Hoffmeier, "Egyptologists," 197–208; Hoffmeier, "Exodus and Wilderness," 46–90; Hoffmeier, *Ancient Israel*; Hoffmeier, "Understanding Hebrew," xxi–xxvii; Hoffmeier, *Israel in Egypt*; Hoffmeier, "Evangelical Contribution," 77–89; and Hoffmeier, "Structure of Joshua 1–11," 165–79.

21. Some of Kitchen's more relevant works on the topic of the Bible and history include: Kitchen, "External Textual Sources—Neo-Hittite," 365–68; Kitchen, "External Textual Sources—Egypt," 369–80; Kitchen, "External Textual Sources—Early Arabia," 381–83; Kitchen, "Hieroglyphic Inscriptions," 117–34; Kitchen, *On the Reliability*; Kitchen, "Controlling Role," 111–30; Kitchen, "Possible Mention," 29–44; Kitchen, "Genesis 12–50," 67–92; Kitchen, "Patriarchal Age," 48–57; Kitchen, "Philistines," 53–78; Kitchen, *Ancient Orient*; Kitchen, "Aramaic of Daniel," 31–79; and Kitchen, "Some Egyptian Background," 4–18.

22. Wiseman's important contributions include: Wiseman, *1 and 2 Kings*; Wiseman, *Nebuchadrezzar*; Wiseman, "Is It Peace," 311–26; Wiseman, "Abraham Reassessed," 141–60; Wiseman, "Jonah's Nineveh," 29–52; Wiseman, "Abraham in History Part 2," 228–37; Wiseman, "Abraham in History Part 1," 123–30; Wiseman, "Archaeology and Scripture," 133–52; Wiseman, "Some Historical Problems," 9–18; Wiseman, *Assyria and Babylonia*; Wiseman, "Rahab," 8–11; and Wiseman, "Archaeological Confirmation," 301–16.

23. Millard's important contributions include: Millard, "Aramaic," 113–21; Millard, "Deuteronomy," 3–15; Millard, "Hebrew Seals," 183–91; Millard, "Daniel in Babylon," 263–80; Millard, "Are There Anachronisms," 39–48; Millard, "Ramesses," 305–12; Millard, "Assyrians," 203–14; Millard, "David and Solomon's Jerusalem," 185–200; Millard, "Were the Israelites," 156–68; Millard, "Tablets," 254–66; Millard, "Value and Limitations," 9–24; Millard, "History and Legend," 103–10; Millard, *Reading and Writing*; Millard, "How Reliable," 50–57; Millard, "Knowledge of Writing," 317–26; Millard, "Owners," 129–33; Millard, "King Solomon," 30–53; Millard, "Assessing Solomon," 25–29; Millard, "Story, History and Theology," 37–64; Millard, "Texts and Archaeology," 19–27; Millard, "Israelite and Aramean," 261–95; Millard, "Mesopotamia and the Bible," 24–30; Millard, "Sign of the Flood," 63–69; Millard, "Statue from

I discovered something interesting as I read the work of these evangelical scholars, who formed a part of what some (including Hoffmeier) have labelled "maximalists," in contrast to the more "minimalistic" scholars who evince more skepticism toward the Bible in regard its historical value. It became quite clear to me, as Hoffmeier has pointed out:

> One reason for the disparity between historical maximalists and minimalists is that the former tend to be trained in Near Eastern languages, history, and archaeology with the Hebrew Bible as a cognate discipline, whereas the latter are largely trained in Old Testament studies in the nineteenth-century European mold and treat cognate languages and sources as ancillary rather than central to their discipline.[24]

This was the impression I was getting. So many of the influential, but skeptically-minded, or minimalistic, scholars I was reading, were primarily biblical scholars trained in the literary methods of modern historical biblical criticism, whereas the evangelical scholars I was reading (as well as Jewish scholars like Gordon) were primarily trained in ancient Near Eastern history and languages. These latter scholars treated the Bible historically much as they did other ancient Near Eastern historical and related documents.

Yamauchi's PhD was not in Bible from some evangelical seminary, but rather was in Mediterranean Studies from Brandeis University.[25] James Hoffmeier's PhD was in Egyptology from the University of Toronto.[26] Kenneth Kitchen, although never completing his PhD, studied Egyptology and Archaeology at the University of Liverpool where he became their most prominent

---

Syria," 135–41; Millard, "Wandering Aramean," 153–55; Millard, "Methods of Studying," 43–58; Millard, "Text of the Old Testament," 27–39; Millard, "Persian Names," 481–88; Millard, "Daniel 1–6," 67–73; Millard, "Assyrian Royal Names," 1–14; Millard, "Practice of Writing," 98–111; Lambert and Millard, *Atrahasis*; Millard, "New Babylonian," 3–18; and Millard, "Recently Discovered," 4–10.

24. Hoffmeier, *Israel in Egypt*, 15.
25. See, e.g., Yamauchi, *Asian American*.
26. See, e.g., Hoffmeier, *Israel in Egypt*, ix.

Professor of Egyptology.[27] Donald Wiseman, after becoming the first student to specialize in both Hebrew and Akkadian at King's College, and earning his Master's at Oxford continuing his study of both Hebrew and Akkadian, became Professor of Assyriology at the University of London's prestigious School of Oriental and African Studies; though he never earned a doctoral degree, the University of London granted him one based on his extensive publications.[28] Millard had been one of Wiseman's master's students in Assyriology at the University of London, after he had already studied Semitics at Oxford, and he was Professor of Hebrew and Semitic Languages at the University of Liverpool.[29]

My exposure to such work, coming from the field of ancient Near Eastern studies, which readily affirmed the substantial historical trustworthiness of the Bible, precisely *as* a collection of ancient historical documents, shaped how I approached such texts. I increasingly became more disposed to reading the Bible against the backdrop of what ancient Near Eastern scholars were learning about the ancient Near Eastern milieu in which the biblical books were written, and I became increasingly less disposed to the many hypothetical literary theories that dominated the discipline of biblical studies.

When I commenced graduate studies in Catholic Theology, focusing on Biblical Studies, at the University of Dayton, I began reading Catholic biblical scholarship more intensely in the standard academic journals, as well as reading books by the standard and most prestigious Catholic biblical scholars. I was confused at how dominant the hypothetical and internal theories of historical biblical criticism (Source, Form, and Redaction) were among Catholic scholars. From about World War II until approximately 1972, there was an increasingly broad positive

27. See, e.g., Kitchen, *In Sunshine*. Kitchen began a doctoral dissertation pertaining to "Western Asiatic lexemes in Ancient Egyptian." See, e.g., Kitchen, "Hieroglyphic Inscriptions," 117.

28. See, e.g., Millard, "Donald John Wiseman," 379–93; and Wiseman, *Life Above*.

29. See, e.g., Block, "Editors' Preface," xv–xvii; and Block, introduction, xxix–xxxiv.

assessment that the Old Testament, at least, was overall a fairly trustworthy picture of the history of the time. That view began to change rapidly after the 1974 publication of Thomas Thompson's book, originally his rejected doctoral dissertation, *The Historicity of the Patriarchal Narratives*.[30]

To me, despite the excessive conclusions of the earlier generation of archaeologists, like W. F. Albright and Gordon, the more cautious but positive conclusions of the next generation of their students—like Yamauchi et al.—seemed to make far more sense of the data than the extreme skeptical positions of scholars like Thompson, or even the more moderate revisions of the literary theories of nineteenth century scholars like Julius Wellhausen that were still reigning in the academic discourse. What was it that drove these nineteenth century scholars like Wellhausen to devise literary theories so untethered to the historical record? Granted, archaeology and, in some cases, the decipherment of some of these languages, was still in its infancy by the end of the nineteenth century.[31] But what explains the dominance of such methods among Catholics especially in the latter half of the twentieth century? These questions were ever in my thoughts during graduate school and as I pursued my doctoral courses at the University of Dayton.

Studying with Portier helped open my eyes to the political and related philosophical and theological influences in both theology and biblical studies, of which, up until that point, I had basically been completely unaware. In his "Methods for the Study of Theology" course, Portier made an off-hand reference to the Frankfurt School and the critical theories of Max Horkheimer and Theodor Adorno. None of us had ever heard of them. This sparked one of the most memorable lectures I ever heard Portier give—and it was off the cuff, completely impromptu. So motivational and inspirational was his lecture, sparked by his incredulity

---

30. Thompson, *Historicity*. Important discussions on this scholarly shift are included in, e.g., Hoffmeier, *Israel in Egypt*, 3–7 and 13–14; Yamauchi, "Current State," 8–11 and 21–25; and Yamauchi, *Scriptures and Archaeology*, 1–4.

31. Though see Machinist, "Road Not Taken," 469–531, for Wellhausen's expertise in Akkadian and the then new discipline of Assyriology, which he consciously chose to ignore in his Old Testament studies.

of our ignorance of the Frankfurt School, that I devoured Horkheimer and Adorno's *Dialectic of Enlightenment* in English over that first Christmas break.[32]

Portier exposed us to other works as well, in his lectures. Few of us had read the work of Alasdair MacIntyre. From Portier's regular references to MacIntyre, I was inspired to read *After Virtue*, *Whose Justice? Which Rationality?*, and *Three Rival Versions of Moral Enquiry*.[33] We read Stanley Hauerwas' Gifford Lectures, *With the Grain of the Universe* in class.[34] This led me later to read other works by Hauerwas, including especially *The State of the University*,[35] and other related texts, like Gavin D'Costa's *Theology in the Public Square*.[36] In his doctoral seminar, "God and the State," Portier had us read from Hauerwas' student William Cavanaugh. We read his ground-breaking article, "'A Fire Strong Enough to Consume the House': The Wars of Religion and the Rise of the State," and his later "Killing for the Telephone Company: Why the Nation-State is Not the Keeper of the Common Good."[37] All of these works, and others, helped me see the often ignored political context to some of the theological conversations we were having.

John Milbank's influential but controversial *Theology and Social Theory*, which Portier also had us read in class, was of momentous importance to me.[38] Milbank included a very brief but eye-opening subsection titled, "Modern Politics as Biblical Hermeneutics,"[39] in which he wrote, "It was . . . necessary for the new political science to 'capture' from Catholic Christianity

32. The version I read was Horkheimer and Adorno, *Dialectic*. For a more recent English edition see Horkheimer and Adorno, *Dialectic*, ed. Noerr.

33. MacIntyre, *After Virtue*; MacIntyre, *Whose Justice*; and MacIntyre, *Three Rival Versions*.

34. Hauerwas, *With the Grain*.

35. Hauerwas, *State of the University*.

36. D'Costa, *Theology*.

37. Cavanaugh, "Fire Strong Enough," 397–420; and Cavanaugh, "Killing for the Telephone Company," 243–74. This work was later expanded into Cavanaugh, *Myth of Religious Violence*.

38. Milbank, *Theology and Social Theory*.

39. Milbank, *Theology and Social Theory*, 17–20.

the text of the Bible: to produce a new Biblical hermeneutic."[40] Milbank identified the early modern political theorists Thomas Hobbes and Baruch Spinoza as key figures in this transformation into modern biblical criticism, underscoring political motivations.[41] At the same time I was reading Jon Levenson's *The Hebrew Bible, the Old Testament, and Historical Criticism*.[42] Like Milbank, Levenson also identified Hobbes and Spinoza (and Richard Simon) as foundational for the development of modern biblical criticism.[43] Moreover, Levenson pointed out how "historical criticism is the form of biblical studies that corresponds to the classical liberal political ideal. It is the realization of the Enlightenment project in the realm of biblical scholarship."[44] This was consistent with, albeit different from, what I had learned from Yamauchi, as when he wrote, "Modern biblical criticism has been characterized by anti-supernaturalism."[45]

As a doctoral student, as I examined twentieth century debates about Catholic biblical scholarship, for example the published exchange between Luke Timothy Johnson and Roland Murphy, I found myself going back to the controversies surrounding Pope Pius XII's 1943 *Divino Afflante Spiritu* and Pope Leo XIII's 1893 *Providentissimus Deus*.[46] This eventually made me aware of the work of Alfred Loisy and Marie-Joseph Lagrange. This context helped me better understand the emergence of Catholics embracing modern historical biblical criticism after the Second Vatican Council.

Most of my work since graduating from Dayton has been uncovering the seventeenth through nineteenth century roots of

40. Milbank, *Theology and Social Theory*, 17.
41. Milbank, *Theology and Social Theory*, 17–20.
42. Levenson, *Hebrew Bible*.
43. Levenson, *Hebrew Bible*, 117.
44. Levenson, *Hebrew Bible*, 118.
45. Yamauchi, "Current State," 5.
46. E.g., Johnson, "What's Catholic," 3–34; Johnson, "So What's Catholic," 12–16; Murphy, "Historical Criticism," 4 and 29; Murphy, "What Is Catholic," 112–19; and Johnson, "Crisis," 18–21.

modern biblical criticism in figures like Thomas Hobbes, Baruch Spinoza, Richard Simon, and the lesser known friend of Simon's, Isaac La Peyrère.[47] As I engaged in more detailed studies of these figures, I continued to read widely in the history of biblical scholarship through the eighteenth, nineteenth, and twentieth centuries as well.[48] One area of interest for me has been the reception of modern biblical criticism, particularly historical criticism, in the Roman Catholic world.

My Interest in Roman Catholic Modernist Studies

By the 1970s, and certainly today, some of the leading biblical scholars and historical critics have been Catholics, and yet, this had not always been the case. The twentieth-century's towering giants of modern biblical scholarship, like Raymond Brown and Joseph Fitzmyer, had difficult battles to fight as they became recognized as leading biblical scholars. In light of Pius IX's *Syllabus of Errors*, and Pius X's *Pascendi Dominici Gregis*, not to mention the many early decisions of the Pontifical Biblical Commission, mainstream biblical scholars, primarily coming from mainline Protestant denominations, initially viewed Catholic biblical scholars with suspicion, assuming they were not free to think for themselves and engage in open and honest critical inquiry. Scholars like Brown and Fitzmyer had an uphill battle proving themselves as scholars, which they did quite successfully and admirably.[49]

Within this history, the controversy over modernism proves pivotal. On the one hand, Loisy and his contemporaries like

---

47. E.g., Morrow, "Bible in Captivity," 285–99; Morrow, "Early Modern," 7–24; Morrow, "French Apocalyptic," 203–13; Morrow, "*Leviathan*," 33–54; Morrow, "Pre-Adamites," 1–23; Morrow, "Spinoza's Use," 1–18; Morrow, "Faith, Reason and History," 658–73; Morrow, *Three Skeptics*; Morrow, "Acid of History," 169–80; Morrow, *Theology, Politics, and Exegesis*; Morrow, "Spinoza and the Theo-Political," 374–87; Morrow, *Pretensions of Objectivity*; and Morrow, "Methods of Interpreting," 157–73.

48. Hahn and Morrow, *Modern Biblical Criticism*.

49. Morrow, "Fate of Catholic," 54–55; and Johnson, "What's Catholic," 11–15.

Lagrange, were really at the forefront of Catholic engagement with modern biblical criticism. On the other hand, the climate after Pius X's condemnation of modernism was inimical to such biblical scholarship. To the first point, regarding the revolutionary methods during and just prior to the modernist controversy, typically it is asserted that before the work of figures like Lagrange and Loisy, Catholics ignored modern historical biblical criticism, except for the artificially constructed apologetics used to inoculate against such higher criticism, as in Fulcran Grégoire Vigouroux's courses. In the light of Ulrich Lehner's work on the Catholic enlightenment, such an absolute position is no longer tenable.[50] Lehner has done an important job showing how a number of prominent, mostly German, Catholic biblical scholars were engaged in modern biblical criticism, particularly in the eighteenth century, and learning from such figures as Johann David Michaelis at the University of Göttingen. And yet, the exceptions like those Lehner brings attention to, in some regard prove the rule, and his work has shown the censorship and sometimes condemnation such critical scholarship received officially.

In general, Catholic exegetes did not engage in what was then still primarily German biblical criticism, granting the exceptions Lehner showcases. Part of the reason for this perhaps was the result of the seventeenth century condemnation of Simon's works in this regard, which cautioned Catholics from moving in the historical-critical direction, as well as the condemnations others in the eighteenth century received.[51] Moreover, such studies, primarily produced in English and German, became quickly associated with Spinoza, who was regularly condemned for so-called pantheism, or panentheism, or often atheism, in Catholic circles.[52] In general such approaches were denounced as rationalist.

50. E.g., Lehner, *On the Road*, 193-330; Lehner, *Catholic Enlightenment*, 14-70; and Lehner, *Enlightenment Monks*.

51. See, e.g., the discussion in Lehner, *On the Road*, 239-78.

52. On the importance of the reception of Spinoza in this regard throughout especially the seventeenth and eighteenth centuries, see, e.g., Israel, *Radical Enlightenment*; and Israel, *Enlightenment Contested*.

To the second point, regarding the hostile climate in the wake of *Pascendi*, one need only turn to François Gigot's popular seminary textbook, *General Introduction to the Study of the Holy Scriptures*,[53] thoroughly engaging with the standard historical criticism of the day and compare it with his anemic defense of the Mosaic authorship of the Pentateuch after modernism's condemnation.[54] Teaching in Dunwoodie, New York, at St. Joseph Seminary, Gigot would doubtless have been aware of the publications in *Princeton Theological Review* which were making waves, many of which included far more persuasive arguments in favor of the traditional view Gigot was apparently supporting.[55] In a short time more robust arguments would emerge challenging Wellhausen's and related Documentary Hypotheses as explanations for the composition of the Pentateuch. Three that come to mind from the first half of the twentieth century are the works of Augustin Bea in 1928,[56] which focused on internal arguments concerning style, Umberto Cassuto in 1934,[57] which focused on the Hebrew language and style in light of other ancient Near Eastern languages and literatures, and Yehezkel Kaufmann from 1937–1956,[58] which focused on the antiquity of priestly material and the archaeological record.[59]

---

53. Gigot, *General Introduction*.

54. Gigot, *Message of Moses*.

55. See, e.g., McPheeters, "Question of Authorship of Books," 362–83; McPheeters, "Question of Authorship," 579–96; and Boyd, "Ezekiel," 29–51.

56. Bea, *De Pentateucho*.

57. Cassuto, *La questione*.

58. Here I am referring to Kaufmann's 8 volume work, *Religion of Israel*, published in Hebrew. An abridged version is available in English as Kaufmann, *Religion of Israel*.

59. In addition to these Catholic and Jewish scholars, there were a host of self-identified Fundamentalist Protestant scholars, like Robert Dick Wilson, mainly from Princeton Theological Seminary, who published rather erudite articles challenging the Documentary Hypothesis, e.g., in addition to those cited above, Wilson, "Use of 'God,'" 644–50.

I have met a number of evangelical biblical scholars and archaeologists, like Yamauchi, Charles Aling,[60] Hoffmeier, et al., none of whom would be persuaded by Gigot's arguments, and yet they all attribute the Pentateuch primarily to Moses.[61] I think Gigot's change can be accounted for by the 1908 excommunication of Loisy, the 1909 dismissal of Henry Poels from teaching at the Catholic University of America, as well as the general climate of suspicion and fear that was created by anti-Modernist institutions envisioned in *Pascendi* and like the Sodalitium Pianum. As Marvin O'Connell explains, the Sodalitium Pianum "provided an opportunity for all those who cared to label as Modernists their bishops, parish priests, professors, local editors, or indeed anyone with whom they disagreed. No one was safe."[62] In such a context, such biblical criticism was stifled among Catholic exegetes and would be forced to wait another generation before being engaged publicly by Catholics.

So, Roman Catholic modernism's pivotal place within the history of Catholic appropriation of modern historical biblical criticism fits neatly within my own research agenda. Beyond this, however, my own interest in modernism is partly autobiographical. As a convert from Judaism to Catholicism, many of the issues I wrestled with were issues like those the modernists dealt with too; issues pertaining to the relationship between faith and reason, the subjective knower and the objective known, history and the development of doctrine, etc. My Jewish upbringing was not that of my parents, nor of their parents, but was firmly entrenched in the world of American religious pluralism. Passing briefly

---

60. Aling earned his PhD in Egyptology from the University of Minnesota, and has published a number of relevant works in this area, including: Aling, "Some Remarks," 31–37; Aling, "Biblical City," 129–37; Aling, *Egypt and Bible History*; and Aling, "Sphinx Stele," 97–101.

61. Some of their works challenging the Documentary Hypothesis include Yamauchi, *Composition and Corroboration*; Aling, *Egypt*; and Hoffmeier, *Ancient Israel*.

62. O'Connell, *Critics on Trial*, 363. See Fogarty, *American Catholic*, especially the endnotes, for the ways in which this type of biblical scholarship was driven underground during this time.

through evangelical Protestantism en route to Catholicism, in some ways I resemble Portier's description of "evangelical Catholics" in his 2004 "Here Come the Evangelical Catholics."[63] Dates like 1968 did not serve as identity-markers for me; I would not be born for another full decade. And yet, I began to see how the experiences of my teachers and of their teachers in the post-1968 world of academic Catholic theology of the 1970s and 1980s, mirrored, in some ways, many of the same issues raised in the modernist conflict at the dawn of the century.[64] In reading about that much earlier conflict, I was in some sense learning more about my own teachers, and their senior colleagues and teachers. Portier captures well the perils of studying these figures:

> The modernist crisis makes the self-involving nature of theological inquiry unavoidable even to the obtuse. Remembering the modernist crisis takes on a certain moral cast that puts the inquirer at risk. One is drawn to take sides and to consider one's obligations.[65]

For me, studying modernism has taken on a very personal nature. Even if I do not recognize myself in the figures I study, I do recognize some of my teachers and some of their colleagues, whom I count among my friends.

Alfred Loisy and Modern Biblical Studies

My own work, *Alfred Loisy and Modern Biblical Studies* is composed of seven chapters. In the first chapter I take a look at the history of the modernist conflict, and I situate Loisy within that context. Of course, the conflict that erupted during the papacy of Pius X had roots which preceded his papacy; and this is true both of those accused of modernism as well as of the anti-modernists. I look at some of the intellectual and political roots of the conflict, and some

---

63. Portier, "Here Come," 35–66.

64. The personal reflections in Portier, "Jesus and the World," 374–96 is helpful here.

65. Portier, *Divided Friends*, 39.

of the proximate historical antecedents. Three of the chapters, specifically chapters two, three, and seven, began as papers presented before La Société, at Talar's gracious invitation.[66]

In the second chapter I depart from the story of modernism and of Loisy, and discuss the history of the discipline of Assyriology, which is the study of ancient Mesopotamia (mainly ancient Assyria and Babylon). This academic field was relatively young in Loisy's day. My reason for taking this step back to look over the history of the development of Assyriology is that I wanted to discuss the origins of the field before taking a look at Loisy's place within that specific discipline. Interestingly, Jules Oppert, one of Loisy's Assyriology thesis readers, is typically heralded as one of Assyriology's founding figures. The France of Loisy's time, at the end of the nineteenth century, was an important seedbed for Assyriology's earliest growth.

From this overview of the history of Assyriology, I turn, in chapter three, to look at Loisy as an Assyriologist. He thus had some things in common with some of my early intellectual influences in biblical scholarship, like Wiseman and Millard. In 2009, Peter Machinist published an important essay on Wellhausen, which he titled, "The Road Not Taken: Wellhausen and Assyriology," in which he discussed Wellhausen's own training in Assyriology, Wellhausen's own consideration of going into that discipline as a primary specialty, but his eventual refusal and selection of different roads.[67] Something similar happened with Loisy, so I

---

66. Chapters two, three, and seven, began as papers for La Société Internationale d'Études sur Alfred Loisy. A version of what became chapters two and three was also presented before the Near Eastern Archaeological Society. Revised editions of those papers were published first in the *Near Eastern Archaeological Society Bulletin*, and a separate version was published in the *Journal of Religious History*. A version of what became chapter seven was eventually published in the *International Journal of Systematic Theology*. Chapter four initially began as a paper for the Nineteenth Century Theology Group of the American Academy of Religion, and was subsequently published in their proceedings, revised and then republished in the *Journal for the History of Modern Theology*. The sixth chapter originated as a paper for the American Catholic Historical Association.

67. Machinist, "Road Not Taken," 469–531.

could have titled my chapter, "The Road Not Taken: Loisy and Assyriology." Loisy's engagement with Assyriology, however, was far more thorough than Wellhausen's, and unlike Wellhausen, Loisy attempted to travel down that professional road. Loisy completed a full graduate curriculum in Assyriology including an unpublished thesis on the Royal Annals of Sargon II. The chair of Assyriology he attempted to secure, however, never materialized.

Next, I turn to look at how his assiduous study of Assyriology impacted Loisy's biblical scholarship by examining his work on the Genesis creation and flood material in light of Babylonian and other Mesopotamian traditions. I show how Loisy combined both a comparative approach utilizing a broad range of ancient Near Eastern materials, with the source critical approaches like those of Wellhausen. At the time, this was an uncommon combination of methodologies.

After this, I take another step back and survey the history of the development of the sort of historical criticism, mainly source criticism, on which Loisy relies. Such criticism has deep roots, but I focus on its development from the seventeenth through nineteenth centuries. Not insignificantly, Loisy relies upon the work of most of the prominent scholars, and even lesser-known ones, within this history. That is, unlike so many of his contemporaries, Loisy not only relies upon the most recent findings from his contemporary historical critical scholars, but he is actually quite familiar with the long tradition of scholarship, of which so many of his own day, and so many today, remain fairly ignorant.

I then turn to the way in which Loisy utilized Richard Simon throughout his works. In Loisy's earliest publications, he relied upon Simon's seventeenth century scholarship as sources, among others, in Loisy's own critical works. When Loisy's own work became controversial, and certainly after his excommunication, Loisy used Simon more as a symbol of his own struggle. The two had many parallels in their biographies. Simon and Loisy were both priest scholars whose works landed them in conflict with the Church's hierarchy. Simon's resulted in his expulsion from the Oratorians, whereas Loisy's resulted in his excommunication. If I had had more time during my sabbatical, when the bulk of the work for this book was completed, I would have expanded this study to include the ways in which Loisy used Bishop Bossuet as a symbol, since he appears to use Bossuet symbolically in reference to Loisy's own contemporary opponents, perhaps especially Cardinal Richard of Paris, but time constraints forced me to limit my study to the work I had already accomplished prior on his use of Simon.

My final chapter examines Loisy's defense of historical criticism within the Catholic world in his pseudonymous "Firmin" articles, focusing on the last of those articles which Loisy expanded into the book, *The Religion of Israel*. I argue that Loisy used the ideas of John Henry Newman on the notion of development of doctrine in order to defend reliance on the historical critical method of biblical exegesis, particularly source criticism. His basic argument was that just as development in doctrine occurred throughout church history, as Newman so powerfully argued, so too there is development within the biblical texts themselves, and within the history lying behind those texts as we now have them. The historical critical method was an essential means of uncovering that historical development evidenced in Scripture.

Conclusion: My Work's Contribution to Modernist Studies

So, what does my book contribute to the study of Roman Catholic modernism? One minor contribution my work makes is that it uncovered an earlier pre-*Pascendi* usage of the notion of "modernism" that sounded very much like what Pius X condemned. It is often assumed that the idea of a nefarious and organized modernism was the invention of Piux X. Although such an organized modernism, as imagined by *Pascendi*, may not have actually existed, that anti-modernist characterization predated Pius X's papacy. Indeed, as early as 1883, when Loisy was working on his theology doctorate, and had only been a priest for about four years, we read the following in an anonymous article in *La Civiltà cattolica* titled, "Modernism" ("Il modernismo"):

> The new paganism, which is called *Modernism*, and more commonly Liberalism or Revolution, also battles the Church; because, as an instrument of Satan, and informed by the same spirit, the hatred of Christ, it is moved by the same end, namely of impeding everyone from the benefit of redemption.[68]

In that article, *Modernism* is capitalized and placed in italics. Notice too it is identified "as an instrument of Satan," and is claimed to be "informed by the same spirit," namely, Satan's. This sounds very much like what we find in *Pascendi*, but it was published over twenty years earlier. In my first chapter I discuss a number of early examples of such pre-*Pascendi* uses of "modernism," although most date from the papacy of Pius X.

More substantially than this minor point, my volume contributes to the study of modernism by situating Loisy's own work within the context of his biblical and ancient Near Eastern studies, which was the main reason I began this project. In my experience, it seems that most scholars of modernism hail from historical theology and/or systematic theology, rather than biblical studies. Moreover, even within biblical studies I find the average Bible scholar woefully ignorant of the history of their own discipline. Obviously, there are significant exceptions to this. What I hoped to do in my own study is take my work in the history of biblical scholarship and situate Loisy within that context. Very few scholars have explored Loisy's biblical work, focusing instead on his more modernist theological writings,[69] or, more recently, in his work in history of religions.[70] Talar is one of the few exceptions with his work on Loisy's biblical scholarship and his studies on Genesis.[71] It is true that Christoph Théobald and François Laplanche have important studies in this regard that include a discussion of Loisy's

---

68. "Il modernismo," 539.

69. Burke, "Was Loisy," 139-57; Turvasi, *Condemnation*; and Wernz, "Loisy's 'Modernist' Writings," 25-45.

70. E.g., Lannoy, *Alfred Loisy*; Praet, "Symbolisme," 127-45; and Lannoy, "Comparing Words," 111-26.

71. Talar, "Between Science," 27-42; and Talar, "Innovation," 191-211.

biblical work, but most of their studies are not focused on Loisy.[72] And yet, Loisy's modernist works, like *L'Évangile et l'Église*, were grounded in his prior work in biblical studies.

What I discovered was that Loisy's work that typically gets associated with modernism often pertains to how he understood doctrinal development within the Bible itself, and particularly with regard to the New Testament. His work in the New Testament, however, was conditioned by his Old Testament studies. My own work and that of Talar's are among the rare ones that really focus on Loisy's early scholarship in the Old Testament.[73] Moreover, it is often mentioned in passing that Loisy studied Assyriology. Perhaps my book's greatest contribution lies in situating Loisy's biblical scholarship in the context of his Assyriological and ancient Near Eastern studies.

Loisy had learned historical criticism primarily from Louis Duchesne's lectures in Church history he attended, from Ernest Renan's lectures on the Bible he audited, and from his own reading in biblical studies, especially initially the work of Édouard Reuss. Loisy's studies in Assyriology at the feet of Arthur Amiaud, primarily, taught him the importance of a comparative approach to the Bible. Loisy learned to study ancient Mesopotamian literature in its original Akkadian, and then make comparisons with comparable stories in the Bible, as he exemplified in his work on creation and flood narratives in Genesis. Thus, whereas Loisy's contemporary scholars tended either to focus their studies on traditional historical criticism, which was primarily on internal literary grounds, or else they focused instead on comparing the biblical material with other discoveries from the ancient Near East, Loisy engaged in both methods. As an adept student of both disciplines, Loisy was well placed to combine these approaches, and he did so with skill.

In the next chapter, I engage the broad work that has been done in modernism throughout especially Europe, but beyond

---

72. See, e.g., Théobald, "L'exégèse catholique," 387–439; and Laplanche, *La Bible en France*.

73. Morrow, *Alfred Loisy*; and Talar, "Between Science," 27–42.

the confines of the Catholic Church. We will see that the ideas that were alive during the Roman Catholic Modernist controversy, were found elsewhere in Europe, in different confessional contexts, as scholars grappled with new findings in history, science, and the field of comparative religion. Many of their works overlapped with one another, and in some cases, as with Franz Cumont and Loisy, after Loisy's excommunication, there was some intellectual collaboration.

2

Modernism Broadly Understood

Introduction

IN THE LAST CHAPTER, we took a look at my own contribution to the study of Roman Catholic Modernism by situating my book on Alfred Loisy's engagement with Assyriological and biblical scholarship within the context of my own academic formation and my scholarly work in the history of modern biblical criticism. In this chapter I take a look at the scholarly discussion of modernism in a broader sense during the late nineteenth and early twentieth centuries, mostly in Europe, but across confessional boundaries. I do this mainly through engaging the important studies of this broader scholarly trend published in Danny Praet and Corinne's significant volume, *Science, Religion and Politics during the Modernist Crisis*.[1]

Scholars of modernism are often held in suspicion by their colleagues. Why would anyone remain interested in that period of time and in those controversial figures from the end of the nineteenth and early part of the twentieth century? Such questions

1. Praet and Bonnet, ed., *Science, Religion and Politics*.

puzzle professional colleagues and students alike. And yet the demise of studies on modernism has been greatly exaggerated. The past decade has witnessed a number of significant studies published on some aspect of modernism (and responses to modernism), and more studies remain forthcoming.[2] Praet and Bonnet's *Science, Religion and Politics during the Modernist Crisis* is another of these studies that makes an important contribution to the study of modernism, particularly in regard to its breadth of focus.[3] The book is divided into three parts and includes fifteen chapters, and I think it will be of benefit to summarize these studies in this format to make its findings available to a broader audience beyond merely specialists. Thus, in what follows I provide brief overviews of each highlighting points throughout this relatively unknown volume that I think are particularly worthy of note.

A number of related edited volumes pertaining to modernism in some form have been published in recent decades.[4] The year 2000 saw the publication of *Il modernismo tra cristianità e secolarizzazione*, whose 38 essays focused on modernism from within the more general framework of the notion of secularization.[5] Although international in scope (including England, the U.S., Spain, France, and Germany), this volume really had more material pertaining to Italy than any other single region. 2010 witnessed the publication of 27 essays in an important German edited volume on modernism and anti-modernism in the context of the Catholic Church, edited by Hubert Wolf and Judith Schepers.[6] Three years later, in 2013, came *Religious Modernism in the Low Countries*, which

---

2. These include: Marshner, ed., *Defending the Faith*; Maher, *Forgotten Jesuit*; Morrow, *Alfred Loisy*; Lannoy, *Alfred Loisy*; Petráček, *Bible and the Crisis*; Schultenover, *Jesuit Superior*; and Arnold, Tacchi, and Vian, *Controversy*.

3. Praet and Bonnet, ed., *Science, Religion and Politics*.

4. In their introduction Praet and Bonnet situate their volume in the context of these other related works, underscoring what is unique about their own work. See Praet and Bonnet, introduction, VII–XXXII.

5. Botti and Cerrato, ed., *Il modernismo*.

6. Wolf and Schepers, ed., *"In wilder"*.

included 15 essays with more of a focus on Belgium (like Praet's and Bonnet's volume), as well as on the Netherlands.[7]

These 95 essays, including those of the present volume, make it clear that the study of modernism (Catholic and beyond) is alive and well. What is unique about Praet and Bonnet's volume is that it deals with the context of modernism outside of simply the Catholic Church and shows how such modernism had an impact on other areas of European culture, on specific individuals, and on society as a whole, focusing on the political, scientific, and scholarly religious context instead of simply the ecclesiastical context. As the Praet and Bonnet mention at the outset, "This book studies the relationship between science, religion and politics during the Modernist crisis," and it does so looking first at the international context, then more narrowly in the context of Belgium, and finally, focusing on the more specific Belgian conflict over Franz Cumont.[8] Those contexts form the three parts into which the book is neatly divided.

Pascendi Dominici Gregis (1907)

Giacomo Losito's essay focuses on Pope St. Pius X's 1907 anti-modernist encyclical *Pascendi Dominici Gregis*.[9] This encyclical represented the Magisterium's most forceful condemnation of modernism. What makes Losito's contribution unique and especially worthy of comment is his specific focus on the impact *Pascendi* had on the education of priests in France at the time. This has been an understudied area regarding *Pascendi*'s impact and influence. What Losito's study demonstrates is how, in the wake of *Pascendi*, seminary students in France were no longer able to take any of their courses at state-run institutions.

Education at state-run institutions became such an important issue, even for French anti-modernists, in part because the only

---

7. Kenis and van der Wal, ed., *Religious Modernism*.
8. Praet and Bonnet, introduction, VII.
9. Losito, "État, Église et Université," 3–48.

place for French academics to receive teaching licenses were state institutions, the very ones Catholic clerics could no longer attend. Precisely because of this, as one might expect, in most contexts, exceptions were made out of necessity. One thing Losito's study of this conflict does is show how interwoven secular and ecclesiastical debates were in the France of the time, even after the Laws of Separation of 1905. It also shows the deep divisions within Catholicism of the time, even within the Catholic anti-modernist hierarchy. Scholars of modernism have long argued that modernists were not monolithic. It becomes clear, in light of studies like Losito's study, that neither were the anti-modernists monolithic.

Salomon Reinach and the History of Religions

Charles Talar's chapter comes next in Praet and Bonnet's volume.[10] Talar examines Salomon Reinach within the context of the history of religions. Reinach's most important work on the history of religions was his 1907 textbook *Orpheus*.[11] One key move Reinach makes in *Orpheus* is his inclusion of Christianity as just one among other of the world religions. This has the natural effect of at least partially relativizing Christianity and any truth claims it might make. This was one of the points of some studies of the history of religion that likewise examined Christianity using the same methodological paradigms and lenses as other religious traditions, and, indeed, one of the focal points in the very creation of the category of "religion" itself as something separable and abstract that can be an independent object of study.

Talar's contribution examines the reception of *Orpheus* from a wide-range of perspectives, including both Catholic and non-Catholic vantage points. Those intellectuals who responded to Reinach's work ranged from positive appreciation to defensive critique, as well as in-between those two poles. Talar's concluding

---

10. Talar, "Salomon Reinach's *Orpheus*," 49–71.
11. Reinach, *Orpheus*.

remarks illuminate the importance of the historical context in this discussion when he writes:

> The Separation of Church and State in 1905 and its contentious aftermath, coupled with debates over instruction in a *morale laïque* in an increasingly secularized society raised the stakes where exposure to the history of religions was at issue. It was into this context that Reinach launched *Orpheus* and it is little wonder that the book evoked the number of extensive responses it did.[12]

The Philosophical Specter of Kant

François Trémolières takes up the philosophical context of *Pascendi* as the main topic of his.[13] He argues that much of the conflict between modernists and anti-modernists was epistemological in nature. He points out how *Pascendi* evidenced a fear of using Immanuel Kant's epistemology and thereby banishing Catholicism to the inner recesses of individual subjectivity.[14] In his survey of twentieth-century Catholic theology, Fergus Kerr noted the paradox, stretching back to Pope Leo XIII but including Pius X's *Pascendi*, that such magisterial directives "intended to keep modern philosophy out of Catholicism . . . kept to very much the same canons of rationality as we find in the Enlightenment."[15]

---

12. Talar, "Salomon Reinach's *Orpheus*," 68–69.

13. Trémolières, "Au confluent," 73–98.

14. On this topic, namely, the important place of Kant behind the debates over modernism, see also, Mansini, "Experience and Discourse," 1131 and 1134–38; Colin, *Morale et religion*, 49–56; Talar, "French Connection," 57 and 59–63; Daly, "Theological," 92–96; Colin, *L'audace et le soupçon*, 201–25; and Colin, "Le Kantisme," 9–81.

15. Kerr, *Twentieth-Century*, 2. He continues on the same page, "The Enlightenment ideal was to attain timeless, universal and objective conclusions by exercising a unitary and ahistorical form of reasoning." It would be interesting to read *Pascendi* and related anti-modernist magisterial texts in light of Alasdair MacIntyre's discussion of rationalities in MacIntyre, *Three Rival Versions* and see if they fit better MacIntyre's category of encyclopedic rationality or tradition. MacIntyre uses Leo XIII's *Aeterni Patris* as the textual exemplar of his category of tradition, which Kerr associates more with the canons of

Trémolières shows how *Pascendi* evinces a real fear of what John Milbank calls "methodological atheism"; that is engaging in a field of study or enquiry in practice as if God does not exist, where the scholarly disciplines function in such a way as to be hermetically sealed off from theology's influence.[16] This explains in part why anti-modernists were so concerned with the history of religions, as Talar showed in his previous chapter on Reinach's *Orpheus*. This also explains, according to Trémolières, why *Pascendi* apparently only supported the scholastic approach to theology as opposed to any sort of positive approach or mystical approach, whereas Trémolières maintains all three had been traditional approaches since medieval times.

Pascendi's concern was in part that those historical studies of Scripture and theology that were methodologically atheistic in approach eviscerated Sacred Scripture and the Church's doctrinal tradition. Such scholarship relativized both Scripture and doctrine and thereby endangered the souls of the faithful. Trémolières concludes the remaining portion of his chapter by discussing Neo-Thomistic engagements with the mystical tradition, from the more anti-modernist Neo-Thomist perspective of Réginald Garrigou-Lagrange, on the one hand, to the more closely aligned to *la Nouvelle Théologie* approach of Marie-Dominique Chenu, who ironically had been a student of Garrigou-Lagrange.[17]

French Lay Intellectuals

Claire Toupin-Guyot's contribution to Praet and Bonnet's volume focuses on France. Toupin-Guyot specifically takes a look at the French lay intellectuals who reflected on the challenges of

---

Enlightenment rationality (which he describes in a similar way to MacIntyre's encyclopedic rationality). For a helpful analysis of Kerr's volume that covers much of these topics putting them in a broader context, see Portier, "Thomist Resurgence," 494–504.

16. Milbank, *Theology and Social Theory*, 253.

17. For more recent work on this latter context see Kirwan, *Avant-garde Theological Generation*.

tradition and modernity. These intellectuals sought to reconcile the Church with modern intellectual developments, eschewing any dichotomies between faith and reason.[18] An important part of this context was a retrieval of early church history, and particularly the writings of the early church fathers. This intellectual context formed part of what would later be termed the patristic renewal, which was one of the many important renewal movements that led to the Second Vatican Council.

"Modernism" among Swedish Lutherans

Christian Chanel's chapter follows Toupin-Guyot's with a discussion that moves beyond the context of Roman Catholicism and looks instead at "modernism" within the Lutheran Church in Sweden.[19] The overarching issues Chanel examines within the Swedish Lutheran Church were often the same as within the Catholic Church, namely how to navigate relations between theology and modernity, especially with regard to scientific findings, but also as regarded church and state relationships. Chanel's focus is on Nathan Söderblom and his engagement with the Belgian scholar of the history of religions Franz Cumont.

Chanel applies the term "moderniste" to these Swedish Protestants, like Söderblom, but I am not sure this is very helpful. The term "modernist," in the context of the study of Roman Catholic modernism, has often derived its definition from antimodernist magisterial documents, most notably *Pascendi*. It is difficult enough to locate all of the figures so often lumped into this category—figures as diverse as Maurice Blondel, Alfred Loisy, Marie-Joseph Lagrange, and Pierre Batiffol—that any organized movement as *Pascendi* seems to envision, is fairly difficult to see in the sources.

One might go so far as to say that such a movement never existed *as an organized movement* except in the imagination of

---

18. Toupin-Guyot, "L'intellectuel catholique," 99–115.
19. Chanel, "Les sciences de la religion," 117–55.

anti-modernists. I think, at best, the term can be used in general of those, like Loisy and George Tyrrell who adopted it after *Pascendi*, but much like the term "fundamentalist," I am hesitant to apply it broader than those who self-identified with the label.[20] Even within that context, modernism typically referred to Catholic intellectuals who hoped to reform the Catholic Church from within.

The Study of the History of Religions in Japan

Annibale Zambarbieri's fascinating chapter comes next after Chanel's. Zambarbieri's study pertains to a Japanese scholar, thus broadening the geographical focus of modernist studies even further. Zambarbieri specifically focus on the Japanese scholar Anesaki Masaharu. Masaharu is an especially interesting case, not only for being an Asian scholar, but because Masaharu studied under one of the founding figures of the discipline of the history of religions (*Religionsgeschicte*), or the science of religion (*Religionswissenschaft*), or comparative religion Friedrich Max Müller.[21] Masaharu was the scholar who brought the Max Müller-style study of religion to Japan. He was fascinated by modernism and recognized its political implications, which he supported for the purposes of social reform.[22]

Belgian Anti-Modernism

Jan De Maeyer and Leo Kenis's chapter begins the volume's second part, which narrows its focus dealing specifically with modernism in Belgium.[23] They focus on the complex anti-modernist Cardinal Désiré-Joseph Mercier. Cardinal Mercier tried to challenge

20. On some of the problems with contemporary uses of the term "fundamentalist," see, e.g., Portier, "Fundamentalism," 581–98. On the difficulty of defining modernism and modernists see, e.g., Portier, *Divided Friends*, 19–23.

21. On Max Müller's important place within this history see, e.g., Molendijk, *Friedrich Max Müller*.

22. Zambarbieri, "Anesaki Masaharu," 157–76.

23. De Maeyer and Kenis, "La création," 179–92.

modernism, as defined by *Pascendi*, and he saw himself as aligned with the encyclical. Explicitly, he joined Pius X in condemning modernism. At the same time, however, Cardinal Mercier was intent on the creation of a climate of vibrant intellectualism within the Catholic Church in Belgium. In accord with *Pascendi*'s exaltation of Thomism as the official philosophical tradition, Mercier envisioned a Thomism that was more open and diverse than what was enforced elsewhere during the anti-modernist period.[24]

Belgian Biblical Scholars

In the next essay in Praet and Bonnet's volume, Karim Schelkens studies three Belgian scholars, Albin Van Hoonacker, Alphonse Delattre, and Edmond Picard.[25] Reading about Picard and his anti-Semitism reminds me very much of other roughly contemporary scholars like Adolf von Harnack and Friedrich Delitzsch, specifically in Picard's Marcionite desire to remove the Old Testament from the Christian Bible.[26] Schelkens' depiction of Picard, moreover, fits neatly within the anti-Muslim colonial context of the de-Judaizing of Jesus, whom Picard (like so many others of his generation) depicted as an Aryan. Such a colonial context for historical Jesus studies, as Picard's, began in the nineteenth century as Tomoko Masuzawa's important study has shown.[27] Schelkens concludes his discussion of the different approaches Van Hoonacker and Delattre (both of whom were members of the Pontifical Biblical Commission) had in response to Picard and the use of critical methods in biblical scholarship.

---

24. Mercier's discussion of innovation from within the tradition sounds a lot like MacIntyre's discussion of tradition in *Three Rival Versions*.

25. Schelkens, "Le plus aristocratique," 193–220.

26. On this broader Marcionite context see, e.g., Feller, "Specter," 411 and 419–423; Arnold and Weisberg, "Centennial Review of *Die Große*," 45–61; Arnold and Weisberg, "Delitzsch in Context," 37–45; Arnold and Weisberg, "Babel un Bible und Bias," 32–40 and 47; and Arnold and Weisberg, "Centennial Review," 441–57.

27. Masuzawa, *Invention of World Religions*.

Early on in his essay Schelkens lumps together Pius IX's *Syllabus of Errors* and Pius X's *Pascendi Dominici Gregis* and states that, "These papal doctrines would remain the blueprint of an overall defensive and, at times, outright aggressive ecclesiastical style, one that would only be fully abandoned during the Second Vatican Council."[28] From my own studies I think a bit more nuance is necessary here. On the one hand, although I cannot be certain, my suspicion is that Schelkens would recognize some of the "ecclesiastical style" of Popes St. John Paul II and Benedict XVI—perhaps even St. Paul VI—as bearing a family resemblance to the "aggressive" style Schelkens identifies in these earlier popes prior to the Second Vatican Council.

At the same time it is difficult to read some of the pre-conciliar papal actions, from Benedict XV's liquidation of the anti-modernist Sodalitium Pianum, to Pius XII's publication of *Divino Afflante Spiritu*, as a part of the "overall defensive and, at times, outright aggressive ecclesiastical style" grounded in Pius IX's *Syllabus of Errors* or Pius X's *Pascendi*. We should bear in mind that Benedict XV himself had been held in suspicion as being a modernist.[29] Rather than what Schelkens writes, it might be more accurate to say that the anti-modernist juridical infrastructure was "only fully abandoned" or dismantled at Vatican II.

Le Muséon and Religious Ethnology

Luc Courtois's essay is next in Praet and Bonnet's volume. Courtois writes about Philémon Colinet. Courtois focuses especially on Colinet's involvement in the beginning of the scholarly journal *Le Muséon*, but also on the 1912 Weeks of Religious Ethnology.[30] Courtois shows how Colinet was concerned about the Weeks of Religious Ethnology. Courtois was specifically concerned that, even though the Weeks of Religious Ethnology had an explicitly

---

28. Schelkens, "Le plus aristocratique," 194.
29. See Portier, *Divided Friends*, 42.
30. Courtois, "Le chanoine," 221–49.

missionary focus, he worried that they might harm the faithful in some way regarding their faith.

La Nouvelle Théologie?

Jürgen Mettepenningen and Ward De Pril's essay, which comes next in the volume, is an attempt to challenge the notion that there ever were such movements as "modernism" or *la Nouvelle Théologie*.[31] In the end they argue that those individuals—like Henri de Lubac and Jean Daniélou—who are associated with *la Nouvelle Théologie*—are not representatives of a return to modernism but rather comprise a *"troisième voie"* ("a third way"), a *via media* between *le modernisme* (modernism) and *l'antimodernisme* (anti-modernism). What is the relationship between figures like Loisy and Tyrrell and their ideas, on the one hand, with *Nouvelle Théologie* theologians is an important question.[32]

Whether they are vilified as modernists, à la Reginald Garrigou-Lagrange, or whether they are upheld as intellectual or spiritual heroes, there are clearly areas of connection. Is this because de Lubac et al. steered a middle way between extremes, between the Scylla of Loisy and the Charybdis of Rafael Merry del Val, Pius X's Secretary of State, or are they a continuation, an extension of the work of those accused of modernism? This is not entirely clear. Upon reading Loisy's three volume memoires, Yves Congar wrote, "From that time on the conviction took form in me, with a very definite critical reaction, that our generation's mission was to bring to effect, *within the Church*, that which was true in the queries and the problems posed by Modernism."[33]

I think there is some merit to Mettepenningen and De Pril's *"troisième voie."* One of my main hesitations in endorsing their conclusion is that Loisy and Tyrrell share a lot that resonates with *la Nouvelle Théologie*, and all of these figures foreshadowed, and

31. Mettepenningen and De Pril, "Via media," 251–77.

32. For a relatively recent discussion of this question see especially Kirwan, *Avant-gard Theological Generation*.

33. Congar, *Journal*, 24.

one might argue in some way influenced, what would emerge later at Vatican II. Maurice Blondel, whom one might call the father or forerunner of *la Nouvelle Théologie*, and whom was also suspected of being a modernist, criticized Loisy in his *Letter on Apologetics* and *History and Dogma*.[34] Were Blondel and Loisy closer, as some anti-modernist critics may have believed? Or, if Blondel and Loisy were significantly different, could those differences be simply attributed to differences in temperament, as some have argued Loisy's differences with Marie-Joseph Lagrange were more a matter of temperament?[35]

In some ways, how we understand modernism will influence how we answer these related questions. For example, was modernism an organized movement? Were the modernists mostly dissembling members of the clergy and lay faithful, trying to destroy the Catholic Church from within? Was what *Pascendi Dominici Gregis* identified and condemned as "modernism" more disparate? The relationship of the thought of these figures—e.g., Loisy, Tyrrell, Blondel, de Lubac, Congar—is not so clear. They were certainly united in many ways: in taking subjectivity seriously; in taking history and historical development seriously; in seeking reform; etc. The precise relationship seems to be a bit more complicated.

Histoire des Religions

Jean-Philippe Schreiber's chapter begins the third and final part of the book, which focuses on "L'affaire Cumont."[36] Schreiber situates the discussion over "l'affaire Cumont" in the broader context of the emerging scientific study of religion in Belgium. In particular, he focuses on the case of the religion scholar Eugène Goblet d'Alviella, and all of the many challenges the emerging discipline

---

34. Blondel, *Letter on Apologetics*. On Blondel see, e.g., Bernardi, "Maurice Blondel," 59–77; Blanchette, *Maurice Blondel*; Bernardi, *Maurice Blondel*; and Izquierdo, *Blondel*.

35. For the interpretation of Loisy's and Lagrange's differences as based mostly on temperament, see Lahutsky, "Paris and Jerusalem," 444–66.

36. Schreiber, "Eugène Goblet d'Alviella," 281–312.

of histoire des religions had in the academy in Belgium. The case of d'Alviella reminded me of the regular challenges my friends and colleagues have in comparative religion departments at state universities like my alma mater Miami University, nestled in rural Oxford, Ohio, the oldest religion department at a state school that received completely public funds.[37]

The questions they regularly have had to face pertain to why have a specific academic discipline focused on the study of religion? If it is to be a secular discipline, not grounded in some specific theological position, then why not just study religion in departments of sociology, history, psychology, anthropology, and maybe philosophy? Religion is already studied in these departments from a secular perspective and, moreover, much of what occurs in comparative religion departments is similar to how religion is treated in these other departments. So what need is there for a specific discipline of comparative religion with its own faculty who specialize in this area?

The questions in nineteenth century Belgium were somewhat distinct from these more contemporary challenges in the American academy. In the nineteenth century, Catholics were suspicious of comparative religion because they were concerned it would erode faith, but other scholars who were less religiously motivated, did not think the topic of religion deserved disciplinary autonomy. Would not such a dangerous topic be better left alone? Or, should it not be studied as part of other disciplines? This is the plight of modern comparative religion, feared by the religious as destructive to religion—and not without reason—and held in suspicion by other academics who think such a subject either does not belong in the classroom setting, or else could better be studied in Psychology and Sociology classrooms. As a Mason and anti-Catholic Protestant, Goblet's comparative approach relativized Christianity, and conceptualized an evolutionary approach to the development of religion.

---

37. See Morrow, "75 Years," 81–87.

Modernism in the Belgian Press

Jan Art's essay studies modernism from a unique angle. Art examines the Belgian Liberal press's response to the emerging modernist crisis.[38] Among other things, Art's essay demonstrates the ways in which the "secular" press in Belgium was not simply a disinterested factual reporting mechanism, but rather represented an "interested" secular press, which was very concerned about ecclesiastical affairs during this time period. Art's essay not only underscores the intense debates that were ongoing in Belgium about the modernist crisis, but also the political context at the Belgian universities, and the University of Ghent in particular.

Franz Cumont

The last three essays are the most closely related to each other of the entire volume. Danny Praet's chapter on Cumont is the first of the three.[39] Praet clarifies the political context behind the L'affaire Cumont. Corinne Bonnet's chapter discusses the background to Cumont's forced resignation from Ghent University, especially the political background that Praet had discussed earlier in his chapter.[40] What makes Bonnet's contribution unique is her detailed examination of the Catholic reception of Cumont's work, especially Marie-Joseph Lagrange's critique and Loisy's engagement.

Annelies Lannoy's essay is the volume's final chapter.[41] Her topic is the not-so-well known 1927 international conference held in honor of Loisy's 70th birthday. The conference theme was the history of Christianity. It was a diverse conference, and what Lannoy's study shows is how disunified those associated with modernism actually were. There were several noticeable absences from the conference, especially Cumont himself. Loisy even expressed concerns that this conference in his honor would become some

---

38. Art, "La crise moderniste," 313–37.
39. Praet, "L'affaire Cumont," 339–402.
40. Bonnet, "L'affaire Cumont," 403–17.
41. Lannoy, "Le Congrès," 419–69.

modernist celebration, instead of what it purported to be, namely, a professional conference studying the history of Christianity from within the discipline of the history of religions.

Conclusion

The essays in this volume do a remarkable job of looking at modernism in the broad context of developments in science, religion—especially the scholarly study of religion—and the various European political contexts that are so often absent from studies of Roman Catholic Modernism. Some essays focus more on one or more of these areas than on all three. All of the essays, however, are of a very high quality, and for this the editors as well as the contributors should be commended. I think Praet and Bonnet's volume demonstrates that scholarship on modernism is alive and well, and that new avenues of research, new angles, are continuing to be opened up to those interested in the various figures and issues that arose during that tumultuous time. One thing this volume does exceptionally well is show how much the modernist crisis affected non-Catholics in Europe in a way of which previously scholars had been unaware. In the next chapter, we will take a more careful look at the relationship between modernism and the emergence of the history of religion, or the comparative study of religion. The specific focus will be on Loisy's role as chair of the history of religion at the Collège de France after his 1908 excommunication from the Catholic Church. It will take Annelies Lannoy's book on Loisy as the point of departure for examining his role in the history of religion.[42]

---

42. Lannoy, *Alfred Loisy*.

3

Modernism and the History of Religion

Introduction

IN THE LAST CHAPTER, we briefly surveyed the broader influence of modernism in Europe, especially Belgium, beyond specifically Roman Catholic Modernism. Much of the discussion revolved around the discipline of the history of religion, or comparative religion, and especially the pioneering work of the Belgian scholar Franz Cumont. Cumont was at the center of the debates over the secular study of religion, mostly ancient religions like Mithraism, in Europe, not limited to Belgium. His work was influential throughout, including the French-speaking scholarly world.

In this chapter, we focus our attention more specifically on the work of Alfred Loisy within the history of religion, which was itself very much influenced by Loisy's correspondence with Cumont. On the one hand, Loisy's work here in the history of religion lies outside of his modernist period. On the other hand, the foundation for his work in the study of ancient religions, including

Christianity, was grounded in his earlier work in the study of the Bible and of ancient Near Eastern religions during his Catholic modernist period.[1] As the last chapter was mostly an engagement with the scholarly edited volume Danny Praet and Corinne Bonnet edited,[2] so this chapter will mostly be an engagement with the important work of Annelies Lannoy on Loisy's place within the development of the discipline of the history of religion.[3]

Alfred Loisy: Chair of the History of Religion

Annelies Lannoy has made a remarkably important contribution to both the study of Alfred Loisy but also to the study of the history of religions with her *Alfred Loisy and the Making of History of Religions*.[4] Her book is incredibly wide-ranging, covering not only Loisy's place within the Modernist controversy, and his early training in Assyriology, but also his famous *L'Évangile et l'Église*, and his work in history of religions. Lannoy covers the complex social and political context (with all of its intricate details) behind both the development of history of religions in France, as well as the prominent chair at the Collège de France to which Loisy would eventually be appointed, the "Christ myth" controversy, the history of sacrifice, as well as the role of religion in public/secular education in France, among other topics.[5]

A number of Lannoy's insights are well worth taking a look at since this is such an understudied area of Loisy's life and work. Lannoy has explored Loisy's work, especially as it has intersected

1. On Loisy's work in biblical studies, and especially ancient Near Eastern studies, see Morrow, *Alfred Loisy*.

2. Praet and Bonnet, ed., *Science, Religion and Politics*.

3. Lannoy, *Alfred Loisy*. See also, e.g., Lannoy, "Le Congrès," 419–69; Lannoy, "Comparing Words," 111–26; Lannoy, "St Paul," 222–39; and Lannoy, "La correspondance," 261–65.

4. Lannoy, *Alfred Loisy*.

5. On Loisy's interest in education in France see also, e.g., Morrow, "Religion and the Secular State," 25–45; Hill, "Loisy's 'Mystical Faith,'" 73–94; and Hill, "French Politics," 521–36.

that of Cumont, through her articles but also through her many presentations before La Société Internationale d'Études sur Alfred Loisy. Lannoy mostly focuses on Loisy's later period, after his 1908 excommunication, and specifically his scholarship in the history of religions. This period falls outside of my own area of focus, which has been Loisy's work in the Bible and the ancient Near East prior to his excommunication. His later work, however, built on the foundation of so much of his prior work in this area.

On a more personal level, I enjoyed Lannoy's study because it brought back fond memories for me of my undergraduate days at Miami University in Oxford, Ohio, where I studied comparative religion, in the history of religions mode, in the oldest department in the United States devoted to the study of religion at a public university that was fully funded publicly—Miami was tied with the University of Iowa for the oldest such department, but Iowa's was partially church funded, whereas Miami's had always been completely publicly funded by the state.[6]

I remember reading Émile Durkheim, E.B. Tylor, James Frazer, Friedrich Max Müller, and others mentioned so prominently in Lannoy's volume, in our course on methods for the study of religion. Moreover, I took many classes from the late Thomas Idinopulos, one of whose edited Brill volumes Lannoy cites throughout her important study. Miami University's Department of Comparative Religion had been shaped by the University of Chicago's pioneering work in the history of religion, which included the work of Mircea Eliade and Joseph Kitagawa, who taught many of our professors, most of whom were University of Chicago graduates.

Loisy, William Robertson Smith, and the Development of the History of Religion

The work of William Robertson Smith was an important pioneer within the nineteenth century development of the history of

---

6. Morrow, "75 Years," 81–87.

religion.[7] He even played an influential role in the development of Durkheim's thinking in regard to religion. Robertson Smith likewise played an important role the popularization of the Old Testament scholarship of Julius Wellhausen; he was arguably the single most important person responsible for bringing Wellhausen into the English-speaking world.[8] Lannoy shows how truly pivotal Robertson Smith's theories on religion were for Loisy's own thinking on the role of sacrifice in religion and culture. It is to Loisy's place within this history that we will focus on this chapter, following Lannoy's lead.

At the outset of her important study, Lannoy clarifies her book's intent, "Our study of Loisy's development as a historian of religions aims to advance new insights on the professionalization of the non-confessional study of religion in the first two decades of the 20th century, and on the way this budding discipline was embedded in religion, politics, and society."[9] I think she does this remarkably well throughout her volume, at least as concerns the study of religion in France, which obviously is an important part of the broader history of the history of religions. Perhaps Loisy was not as influential in the broader global conversations of the history of religions as it unfolded in the twentieth century and into our own, in comparison to Durkheim or F. Max Müller, but Loisy engaged with these important figures and played an important role in field of the history of religions as it unfolded in France in his position of chair in that very discipline at the Collège de France.

L'Évangile et l'Église

Most of what Lannoy discusses in her book, other than her introduction and first chapter dealing with Loisy's *L'Évangile et l'Église*,

---

7. On Smith in this context see, e.g., Jung, "Sociology, Protestant Theology," 335–64; Maryanski, "Birth of the Gods," 352–76; Maier, *William Robertson Smith*; Segal, "William Robertson Smith," 1–12; and Beidelman, *W. Robertson Smith*.

8. Hahn and Morrow, *Modern Biblical Criticism*, 217–25.

9. Lannoy, *Alfred Loisy*, 6–7.

pertains to Loisy's scholarly work after his excommunication when he focuses most of his efforts on the history of religion. His earlier work in Assyriology, which he studied at the École pratique des Hautes études, prepared him for a comparative approach to the incipient history of religions perspective he took in *L'Évangile et l'Église*. Of course, Loisy's real major forays into history of religions would be catalyzed by his friendship with the Belgian scholar of history of religions, Franz Cumont, as Danny Praet's and Lannoy's other works have detailed so well.[10]

In Lannoy's comments on *L'Évangile et l'Église* I think her instincts are correct, as when she writes:

> It is very reasonable to assume that his [Loisy's] emphatic use of "the historical method" should not just be understood as a reply to Harnack's proclaimed purely historical account, but also as an attempt to demonstrate his [Loisy's] scientific credibility to the secular circles which had rejected him . . . At about the time he was writing *L'Évangile et l'Église*, Loisy learned that he was in the running for the bishopric of Monaco . . . The fact that he most probably wanted that appointment, may indeed explain why he adopted a well-articulated apologetic discourse in his book, all the while sticking to the conviction that consistent historical criticism was the future of the Catholic science of religion.[11]

I would go a little further and say that Loisy even developed an apologetic, relying upon Newman, in his "Firmin Articles," and implicitly in *L'Évangile et l'Église*, to defend the use of such historical criticism among Catholics.[12]

---

10. See, e.g., Lannoy, "Le Congrès," 419–69; Praet and Lannoy, "Alfred Loisy's Comparative," 64–96; Lannoy, "Comparing Words," 111–26; Praet, "Symbolisme," 127–45; Lannoy, "St Paul," 222–39; and Lannoy, "La correspondance," 261–65.

11. Lannoy, *Alfred Loisy*, 25.

12. Which is one of the main points in the 7th chapter of Morrow, *Alfred Loisy*.

The Marquise Arconati-Visconti and Her Salon

For me, Lannoy's second chapter is really important for underscoring the social and political context of the study of history of religions in the France of Loisy's day, and at the Collège de France in particular.[13] My own book on Loisy, *Alfred Loisy and Modern Biblical Studies*,[14] would have been greatly improved had I known of the more intricate social and political context that Lannoy details in this chapter, particularly regarding the way in which the study of religion and history were "inextricably intertwined with French politics, society, and culture."[15]

Beyond the various intricacies of Loisy's academic rivals for the chair of history of religions at the Collège de France, of special interest in this chapter is the role of the powerful Marquise Arconati-Visconti and her salon. Arconati's social context proved incredibly influential, particularly because of the way in which she patronized historical research. She gathered around herself a wide-range of influential intellectuals, which reminded me very much of the way in which Queen Christina of Sweden, René Descartes' patroness, was similarly influential in the seventeenth century, with her famous library that functioned like a nineteenth- and twentieth-century salon, gathering intellectuals in an informal social setting.[16]

In regard to Arconati's influence here, Lannoy notes that:

> She royally sponsored the *école laïque* and instituted scholarships . . . she strategically financed a whole series of universities and research institutions (e.g. the Sorbonne, the *Collège*, the *École pratique*) . . . Needless to say that Arconati's money brought her an enormous amount of power over academic decision-making . . . she funded libraries and museum collections, created

---

13. I wrote very briefly on this context, but I was wholly unaware of so much of this important social milieu Lannoy discovered, in Morrow, "Religion and the Secular State," 25–45.

14. Morrow, *Alfred Loisy*.

15. Lannoy, *Alfred Loisy*, 76.

16. See, e.g., Åkerman, *Queen Christina*.

chairs at universities, financially supported scientific journals .... .[17]

Loisy as Scholar and Public Commentator

In her third chapter, Lannoy looks at the way in which Loisy engaged public issues of controversy both in his role as scholar, but also as public commentator, something that was expected of such a prestigious chair as the chair of the history of religions at the Collège de France. One of the main contentious public issues of the day of course was the role, if any, of religion in the secular schools, école laïque, a question in which he had already been engaged prior to his excommunication, on which he wrote pseudonymously.[18]

In looking at Loisy's engagement with and criticism of the comparative history of religions approaches of Durkheim, Salomon Reinach, James Frazer, and the other historians of religion, it is clear that whatever Loisy adopted from them, he did not follow any of them wholesale or uncritically; Loisy consistently challenged their reductionist tendencies. For Loisy, in contrast to so many of these other pioneers in the history of religion, there remained something rich in religious life; religion always retained an important social/moral role. Indeed, Loisy always retained some spiritual language, such that, as Lannoy points out, "it is not very difficult to understand why many scholars—then and now—have believed that Loisy always remained Catholic by heart."[19] Moreover, much as Loisy wished to distinguish between "science" and "religion," he ardently hoped for a peaceful coexistence of both, which hearkened back to earlier humanist aspirations, again perhaps betraying Loisy's Catholic roots.

---

17. Lannoy, *Alfred Loisy*, 100 and 100n114.

18. On his role here see, e.g., Morrow, "Religion and the Secular State," 25–45; Hill, "Loisy's 'Mystical Faith,'" 73–94; and Hill, "French Politics," 521–36.

19. Lannoy, *Alfred Loisy*, 182.

The Different French and German Contexts for the History of Religion

In the context of Loisy's intervention in the Christ myth controversy, Lannoy points to "the very different institutional context of history of religions in France and Germany."[20] She writes:

> Whereas the French *histoire des religions* had a secular character, German *Religionsgeschichte* was embedded in a theological institutional setting. The comparative research of the Göttingen *Schule* was an integral part of a theological commitment for the cultural renewal of Christianity on the basis of historical consciousness.[21]

In light of this background, some questions emerge. In the American context, the German *Religionsgeschichtliche Schule* is often described as wholly secular. And yet, it was unquestionably formed in a Christian, and specifically Protestant, theological institutional context. At the same time, French *histoire des religions*, as secular as it was, strikes me as having some Christian-influenced elements. Even the focus on sacred texts that was often so much a part of both related disciplines' approaches to studying other religious traditions, or what constituted a religion, seems unable wholly to escape in some sense a Christian framework. Tomoko Masuzawa's important work, *The Invention of World Religions: Or, How European Universalism Was Preserved in the Language of Pluralism* shows this to some degree, even as she focuses more on European colonialism.[22]

It would thus be interesting to explore further just how Protestant-influenced, even in Catholic France, these disciplines were, and not only these disciplines, but much of what we

---

20. Lannoy, *Alfred Loisy*, 208.

21. Lannoy, *Alfred Loisy*, 208.

22. Masuzawa, *Invention of World Religions*. Masuzawa uses the example of F. Max Müller and Ernest Renan, both of whom Lannoy also discusses, as prime examples. Lannoy uses Masuzawa's earlier work, *In Search*, but not this more recent work.

consider "secular" disciplines more broadly speaking.[23] This history is reminiscent of the history of the study of Hebrew and of classics at the University of Göttingen, and specifically the work of Johann David Michaelis and the rise of modern biblical studies as a non-theological discipline, in Michael Legaspi's important study on the topic, *The Death of Scripture and the Rise of Biblical Studies*, which was his Harvard University dissertation that Oxford University Press published in 2010.[24] If one does not concede that these are Protestant-influenced, then perhaps at least one could say they are Christian-influenced more generally. Legaspi's more recent work in this area has shown how German Protestant theological and ecclesiastical debates formed an important part of the history behind the rise of the historical critical method in German-speaking academia.[25] Loisy, for one, seemed to retain some vestiges of his Catholic heritage, as evidenced, for example, by his humanist concerns.

The Theological Origins of Modernity

So many have begun to point to "theological origins of modernity." I think here of the work of Charles Taylor and of Michael Gillespie, but so many other works could be added to theirs.[26] Or we could turn to the more controversial work of Andrew Jones' published revision of his Saint Louis University history doctoral dissertation, *Before Church and State*, which implies that the modern so-called secular is an inheritance of medieval Christendom.[27] I think there

---

23. Jones, *Before Church and State*, describes the modern secular as a sort of Christian heresy.

24. Legaspi, *Death of Scripture*.

25. See Legaspi, "Beginnings," 121–42; and Legaspi, "From Thomasius," 11–26.

26. Taylor, *Secular Age*; and Gillespie, *Theological Origins*. See also, e.g., Lehner, *Catholic Enlightenment*; Gregory, *Unintended Reformation*; and Nelson, *Hebrew Republic*.

27. Jones, *Before Church and State*. See my lengthy review, Morrow, "Once There Was," 991–1015.

is some truth to most of these arguments. It strikes me that the ways in which late nineteenth century and early twentieth century scholars of *Religionsgeschichte* and *histoire des religions* operated was very complex, as the case of Durkheim might serve as an example: a secular Jew in a predominantly Catholic France that was in the process of secularizing. Of course, these terms "religion" and "secular" are not without their own problems, but that debate is beyond the scope of my discussion here.[28]

When Lannoy mentions, in the context of the "Christ-myth" debate, that, "Loisy had been primarily concerned with defining the relation between history and myth in such a way that the religious truthfulness of Scripture could be secured,"[29] this was actually quite similar to what early German Protestant biblical scholars had done. Here I am specifically thinking in terms of two scholars who spanned the eighteenth and nineteenth centuries, and whom Loisy utilized in his own works on the Bible: Johann Gottfried Eichhorn and Wilhelm de Wette. As I mentioned in my earlier work on Loisy's use of "myth" in Assyriology and in biblical studies prior to his excommunication, it seems that he was influenced already by the biblical mythic school (represented by scholars like Eichhorn and de Wette), and it would be interesting to examine how much of this influence remained in his later work in history of religions from after his excommunication.

The Jewish Origins of Christianity

Lannoy's work does a good job of showing how Loisy was far more concerned to underscore and understand Christianity's

---

28. For more on the history of the development of these notions see, e.g., Morrow, "Once There Was," 991–1015; Morrow, "Religion and the Secular State," 25–45; Nongbri, *Before Religion*; Cavanaugh, *Myth of Religious Violence*; Feil, *Religio 4*; Asad, *Formations of the Secular*; Feil, *Religio 3*; Feil, *Religio 2*; Harrison, *"Religion"*; Cavanaugh, "Fire Strong Enough," 397–420; Asad, *Genealogies of Religion*; Feil, "From the Classical," 31–43; and Feil, *Religio 1*.

29. Lannoy, *Alfred Loisy*, 214.

Jewish origins than so many of his contemporaries. She explains, for example, how:

> Loisy's entire theory on Christianity can essentially be drawn from this quote: Christianity successfully "transposed" the profoundly Jewish gospel of the historical Jesus into a "beautiful mystery, superior to all others" by exploiting the same oriental mysticism as the mystery cults which were part of its more or less Hellenized environment.[30]

I sometimes wonder how much Loisy's Catholic background made him sympathetic to Jewish sensibilities, much as I wonder how much Durkheim's Jewish background, regardless of how secular he was, made him sensitive to the importance of ritual. Obviously there has been a lot of anti-Semitism within Catholicism. My point is that, in secular, and also in Protestant environments, in the nineteenth century, Judaism and Catholicism were often linked, particularly on the part of intellectuals antagonistic to both traditions.[31] Consider Stanley Hauerwas's astute observation that:

> Catholics understood they often became for Protestants the Jews, that is, Catholics had been surpassed. Nowhere was this more apparent than in the scholarly guilds surrounding the study of scripture in which Second Temple Judaism became the dead priest-ridden religion that the charismatic Christianity of the New Testament replaced. Protestant biblical scholarship simply reproduced that story within their triumph in the Reformation.[32]

Ritual, cult, priesthood, sacrifice, were thus often minimized, or denigrated, as in nineteenth century German biblical scholarship, biblical scholarship in which Loisy was a real expert.[33] Despite all of this, Loisy understood the importance of ritual

---

30. Lannoy, *Alfred Loisy*, 228.

31. This connection is made, for example, in Gross, *War Against Catholicism*.

32. Hauerwas, *State of the University*, 73n46.

33. See the relevant comments, e.g., in Hahn and Morrow, *Modern Biblical Criticism*, 187–225.

within religious traditions in a way that perhaps few outside of the Durkheimians seemed to. This is especially the case in Loisy's discussions on early Christianity.

Loisy's Contested Use of Newman

Before concluding this chapter, I will point out one area of disagreement with Lannoy's fine study. It is an important point, although I do not think Lannoy was pushing it too hard. I mention it in part because she cites my own work in supporting her point with which I disagree, or at least with which I would nuance a bit more.[34] Lannoy stresses Newman's influence on Loisy in regard to the area of the development of doctrine (which Loisy applied to the Bible) a bit too much.[35] I think my assessment here is correct because it is clear that Loisy already had his developmental view firmly in place long before Baron Friedrich von Hügel introduced Loisy to Newman's writings. I think that at most Newman confirmed Loisy's instincts and that Loisy found in Newman a useful ally, rather than being influenced by Newman, as is often thought.[36]

---

34. Lannoy, *Alfred Loisy* cites my own book-length study of Loisy, Morrow, *Alfred Loisy*.

35. This is especially the case in Lannoy, *Alfred Loisy*, 59.

36. See my more complete treatment of this issue in Morrow, "Alfred Loisy's Use," 68–84, e.g., 82, where I summarize, "Any claims that Newmans's works on the development of Christian doctrine provided a sort of breakthrough for Loisy, pushing him in the direction of applying such a developmental approach to the scriptures, overreaches the evidence. In fact, it seems to go against the evidence. Yet, it probably is too facile to limit Newman's role for Loisy to that of a mere rhetorical device ... however, ... he specifically sought someone like Newman—to help provide support for his biblical work ... Loisy seemed to want someone of Newman's stature to help give credence to his own project ... On the one hand, the sort of development Loisy hoped to apply to scripture, he had already been doing for some time. Newman served as an important figure whom Loisy could use both theoretically and rhetorically, to make his argument more amenable to those who might be hesitant to embrace it. It is clear Loisy did not learn about the notion of development from Newman and simply apply it to scripture."

Loisy's "Religion of Humanity" and Its Resonance with Vatican II

For some reason, I was really drawn to Lannoy's last chapter dealing with the religion of humanity and Loisy's studies on the history of sacrifice. I was greatly interested in how Lannoy situated Loisy's (and Cumont's) thoughts on World War I, and the Great War's impact on them. It is in the context of this discussion, particularly of ritual, religion, and sacrifice, that Lannoy mentions the real difference between the Durkheimians and Loisy. She points out how, "Loisy agreed with the Durkheimians on the social function of religion, but he disagreed with their entirely functionalist definition of religion, which he found reductionist."[37] But what really struck a chord in me was the way in which she explained Loisy's historical accounts here in relation to his aspirations for the future of humanity and the centrality of faith.

Following Ivan Strenski, Lannoy underscores Loisy's Catholic-inspired humanist hopes. For Loisy:

> this future fully depended on mankind's commitment to true love, and this true love is for Loisy the equivalent of the willingness to self-sacrifice... within the civil religion Loisy envisioned, sacrifice is seen as a (Christ-like) total self-denial, as the willingness to heroically die for the nation. Loisy's conception of this moral sacrifice is radically different in kind from the ritual sacrifice performed in the religions of history, but the historical links between the two are nevertheless real. In his eyes, it is no coincidence that the same term is used in modern language to indicate the purely moral "gift of self in the performance of one's duty" and the ritual action, the "offering by means of which the security of all is guaranteed by the protection of satisfied divinities."... Loisy explained that the purely moral ideal of altruism and "the gift of the self" ("don de soi") has developed out of ritual sacrifice.[38]

---

37. Lannoy, *Alfred Loisy*, 285.
38. Lannoy, *Alfred Loisy*, 293.

This entire discussion of the "don de soi," the gift of self, called to my mind a famous paragraph from the Second Vatican Council, in its Pastoral Constitution on the Church in the Modern World, *Gaudium et Spes*, namely paragraph 24, where we read:

> Indeed, the Lord Jesus, when He prayed to the Father, "that all may be one... as we are one"... opened up vistas closed to human reason, for He implied a certain likeness between the union of the divine Persons, and the unity of God's sons in truth and charity. This likeness reveals that man, who is the only creature on earth which God willed for itself, cannot fully find himself except through a sincere gift of himself.[39]

I have elsewhere argued that Loisy had published comments in *L'Évangile et l'Église* that were a precursor to Vatican II's teaching on the universal call to holiness.[40] Here, I think we can say something similar about *Gaudium et Spes*' notion of the gift of self. To be clear, I'm not arguing for any direct influence of Loisy on these documents of Vatican II. Rather, I'm arguing that Loisy had certain instincts—and he was not alone here—that would be enshrined in Vatican II.

Lannoy's comments here remind me of a conversation over David Schultenover's massive tome, *Jesuit Superior General Luis Martín García and His Memorias: "Showing Up"*, at a meeting of La Société Internationale d'Études sur Alfred Loisy.[41] Schultenover commented about the way in which Luis Martín, who had been the superior to the Jesuits during the Modernist Crisis, had made a gift of self. Ultimately, this notion of making a gift of self, from a Catholic perspective, is an intrinsic part of what it means to be human, created in the image and likeness of God. For me, Loisy's

---

39. Taken from the Vatican website.

40. Morrow, "Thy Kingdom Come," 3–13, here revised and expanded in chapter 5.

41. Schultenover, *Jesuit Superior*. The conversation took place at a session of La Société Internationale d'Études sur Alfred Loisy alongside the Annual Meeting of the American Academy of Religion in 2021 in San Antonio, TX. The theme of that panel was Schultenover's book. The conversation was between David Schultenover, Stephen Schloesser, Oliver Rafferty, and William Portier.

comments connecting love, self-sacrifice, and the gift of self, represents an important human (and supernatural) contribution to the secular discipline of the history of religions, and a fairly unique one at that. In this way, such a gift of self, we can find a real joy and fulfillment in living out a love for others in the concrete ordinary circumstances of our lives as religious, priests, laity, married, celibate, scholars, or wherever else and in whatever circumstances we find ourselves. Catholic or not, Loisy seemed to retain this important influence from his earlier life, and I think it enriched his scholarship, as secular as it had become.

Conclusion

These last three chapters focused on specific studies of Loisy or of Modernism. The first situated my own volume on Loisy's ancient Near Eastern and biblical scholarship.[42] The second covered the important, yet neglected, scholarly essays in Danny Praet and Corinne Bonnet's edited volume.[43] This chapter took a look at Annelies Lannoy's volume covering Loisy's post-excommunication period of scholarship in the history of religion.[44] The final two chapters of this book will examine Loisy's work in more detail. In the next chapter, we will focus on Loisy's biblical scholarship focusing on his publications prior to his 1908 excommunication in a more detailed way than what I covered in my initial volume on Loisy's biblical scholarship.[45] In this way we will be able to get a better sense of Loisy's early biblical scholarship that led to his eventual excommunication and in fact lay at the heart of the Modernist controversy, as far as the anti-Modernist Catholic Magisterium was concerned.

    42. Morrow, *Alfred Loisy*.
    43. Praet and Bonnet, ed., *Science, Religion and Politics*.
    44. Lannoy, *Alfred Loisy*.
    45. An early version of this chapter was initially published as Morrow, "Études Bibliques," 12–32 and although it was published the year before my book, Morrow, *Alfred Loisy*, my book was completed prior to my commencing work on this article.

4

Alfred Loisy's Early Biblical Scholarship

Introduction

ALFRED LOISY (1857–1940) is perhaps best known for his significant place in the Roman Catholic modernist controversy at the dawn of the twentieth century. Indeed, increasing evidence from the archives of the Vatican have solidified the case that the antimodernist response from the Holy Office of the Inquisition (e.g., its 1907 decree *Lamentabili sane exitu*) and from Pope Pius X was directed in large part against Loisy.[1] What is not always remembered, especially by his critics, is that Loisy was a highly skilled biblical scholar with advanced training in the Bible's broader ancient Near Eastern milieu, including many of the relevant ancient languages (e.g., Akkadian and Egyptian) then available to him.[2]

---

1. See especially Arnold and Losito, ed., *Lamentabili sane exitu*, 303 and 303n347; and Arnold and Losito, ed., *La censure*, 159–60, 159n19, and 160n23. See also the comments in Arnold, "*Lamentabili sane exitu*," 24–51.

2. See Morrow, *Alfred Loisy*.

Lawrence Barmann went too far in his praise of Loisy as, "among Roman Catholic biblical scholars the only one of outstanding distinction,"[3] but this exaggeration helps underscore his real skill that was perhaps rarely matched in his day.[4]

Much of what the anti-modernists viewed as dangerous in Loisy's biblical work became mainstream Catholic biblical scholarship shortly after the mid-twentieth-century. Today, in fact, much of his work would likely be regarded as quaint in circles of contemporary Catholic biblical scholarship in the twenty-first century.[5] It remains the case that Loisy's work in biblical exegesis and history laid the foundation for the works he wrote that would be censured as modernist, e.g., *L'Évangile et l'Église*,[6] and led to his eventual excommunication in 1908.

William Portier aptly explained how the controversy over modernism was "the pivotal opening [to the age] that gives shape to twentieth-century Catholic theology."[7] Considering Loisy's central place within this controversy alone would make an examination

---

3. Barmann, "Pope and the English," 40.

4. That Loisy was in fact not the only Roman Catholic biblical scholar "of outstanding distinction" one need only recall his contemporary Marie-Joseph Lagrange, OP, who was likewise a prolific and highly skilled biblical scholar with more than adequate training in the broader ancient Near Eastern environment in which the Bible originated. On Lagrange see, e.g., Montagnes, *Le Père Lagrange*.

5. My characterization here contrasts with how Nadia Lahutsky characterizes the work of Marie-Joseph Lagrange in comparison to Loisy's: "By today's standards Loisy's critical work sounds eerily contemporary and Lagrange's quaint and traditional . . . Loisy and Lagrange *in their own time* before 1907 were exegetes of what could be called the 'biblical center' and were themselves both attacked by hostile critics on the right and left." See Lahutsky, "Paris and Jerusalem," 445.

6. Loisy, *L'Évangile et l'Église*. This work had its origin in a lengthy unpublished essay, *La crise de la foi dans le temps présent. Essais d'histoire et de critique religieuses*. This unpublished work has now been published as Loisy, "La crise de la foi," 35–491. This lengthy essay was also the seedbed for the articles he published in *Revue du clergé français* from 1898–1900, which he published pseudonymously under his middle name, A. Firmin. On these "Firmin articles" see, e.g., Morrow, "Alfred Loisy's Developmental Approach," 324–44.

7. Portier, *Divided Friends*, 14.

of Loisy's work significant; many consider his 1902 *L'Évangile et l'Église* to have precipitated the modernist crisis. The fact remains that his early works on Scripture remain under examined.[8] Filling the scholarly lacuna of Loisy's scholarly work on the Bible would thus be an important contribution to understanding better the recent history of Catholic theology before and after the Second Vatican Council, since Loisy's work helped set the course for later debates and discussions within Catholic theology.

In the previous chapter I discussed Annelies Lannoy's important contribution to understanding Loisy's place within the development of the discipline of the history of religion in early twentieth-century France.[9] In this chapter I thus hope to contribute to the discussion on Loisy's scholarship and on the history of Modernism through exploring modernism's early pre-history, as it were. The early work of Loisy has been the least explored of his scholarship, thus I examine precisely those understudied early works. Loisy published an incredibly large amount on the Bible throughout his career, even after his 1908 excommunication, and even after his ascending to the chair of history of religions at the Collège de France in 1909.

From my own studies of Loisy's works, I have come to the conclusion that 1893 is the pivotal date prior to his excommunication (which represents another pivotal moment) in his work on the Bible. The year 1893 proves so pivotal not only because of Pope Leo XIII's promulgation of *Providentissimus Deus*, but also because of Loisy's forced resignation on the very day of that encyclical's release.[10] Thus, in this chapter I will consider his works on biblical interpretation and history published up through 1893.[11] I begin

8. Exceptions to this neglect exist, e.g., Morrow, *Alfred Loisy*; and Talar, "Innovation," 191–211.

9. Lannoy, *Alfred Loisy*.

10. For Loisy's own reflections on his studies through this period of time encompassing his dismissal from the Institut catholique see Loisy, *Choses passées*, 53–146; and Loisy, *Mémoires pour server I*, 66–284.

11. There are a few works omitted because I was unable to access them. In most cases I was able to utilize their republished format, since Loisy frequently published books that were collections of his already published journal articles.

with a brief section putting Loisy's work in the context of his life and times. Then I move to a consideration of his major works during this time period. I conclude with some brief comments about the significance of Loisy's early work on the Bible.

The main point of Loisy's early work was the same as that of his later work prior to his 1908 excommunication, namely, to work towards a transformation of Catholic theology via introducing the Catholic world to cutting edge nineteenth-century historical biblical criticism. He did this prior to 1893 with a view toward steering a *via media* between apologetic approaches like those of Fulcran Grégoire Vigouroux (1837–1915)[12] and the more rationalist approaches like those of Joseph Ernest Renan (1823–1892).[13] After 1893, it became crystal clear to Loisy that Church authorities were threatened by his work, and so he took measures to counteract this perception: he wrote more controversial matters pseudonymously; he published differently for his more scholarly audiences; and he published works he intended ostensibly as apologetics, like *L'Évangile et l'Église*, defending against Protestants like Adolf von Harnack (1851–1930), but containing his subtle apologetic for a developmental approach to Scripture.

I was unable to access any of the articles he published in his own periodical, *L'enseignement biblique*. The relevant articles include: Loisy, "Avant-propos," v–xvi; Loisy, "Histoire critique I," 1–76; Loisy, "Histoire critique II," 77–156; Loisy, "Histoire critique III," 157–236; Loisy, "Histoire critique IV," 237–313; Loisy, "Job I," 1–87; Loisy, "Job II," 89–175; Loisy, "De la critique," 1–16; Loisy, "Histoire critique des versions I," 17–80; Loisy, "Histoire critique des versions II," 81–128; Loisy, "Histoire critique des versions III," 129–92; Loisy, "Histoire critique des versions IV," 193–245; Loisy, "Les onze," 1–16; Loisy, "Les *Évangiles*," 17–64; Loisy, "La question du canon," 247–55; Loisy, "Les *Évangiles* I," 1–76; Loisy, "Les *Évangiles* II," 77–156; Loisy, "Les *Évangiles* III–IV," 157–348; Loisy, "La question biblique," 1–16; and Loisy, Évangiles *I*. I had access to the later 1907 version of Loisy, Évangiles *I*, but the two are so different that I am unable to determine what was added. The original was a mere 348 pages, whereas the second edition was more than 1,000 pages.

12. On the significance of Vigouroux see, e.g., Laplanche, *La Bible*, 169–71; and Théobald, "L'Exégèse catholique," 405–9.

13. On the significance of Renan see, e.g., Priest, *Gospel*; and Laplanche, *La Bible en France*, 142–67.

Apologetique Concordiste or Sceptique Rationiste? Loisy's Via Media

Loisy attempted to strike a sort of middle path between the apologetical concordist biblical studies epitomized by Vigouroux and the more rationalist or skeptical position of Renan.[14] Beginning in 1881, Loisy started taking courses in Sacred Scripture from Vigouroux at the Seminary of Saint Sulpice. At the same time, Loisy was studying church history at the feet of Louis Marie Olivier Duchesne (1843-1922), who introduced Loisy to the methods of historical criticism, as applied to early Christian texts. Loisy was both repelled by Vigouroux's courses, which he found both boring and intellectually unsatisfactory. Vigouroux may not have been aware of how his pedagogy affected the young Loisy, but Loisy explained how Vigouroux introduced him to some of the currents in modern historical biblical criticism among primarily German scholars in the course of attempting to refute some of their exegetical and historical conclusions. In the end, Loisy remained unpersuaded by Vigouroux's apologetic refutations, but intrigued by the methods Duchesne introduced.

The following year, in order to go deeper into his study of Hebrew philology and biblical interpretation, and with the permission of his spiritual director, Loisy sat in Renan's courses on the Old Testament and Hebrew exegesis that he taught at the Collège de France. Whereas Vigouroux had only raised the conclusions of historical critical exegetes, and Duchesne had introduced Loisy to the methods applied to early Christian literature, now Loisy witnessed the application of the methods of historical criticism applied to the Bible in Renan's lectures on Hebrew exegesis. In his autobiographical works, Loisy explained his dissatisfaction with Renan's hyper skepticism. In effect, as he explained, Loisy hoped to master Renan's methods in order to use them against him. In his own words: "My ambition was one

---

14. On this see, e.g., Morrow, "Alfred Loisy and les Mythes Babyloniens," 87-103.

day to defeat Renan with his own weapons, through the criticism in which I was instructed at his school."[15]

One of the first things Loisy did to help in this regard was to study Egyptology and throw himself completely into the study of Assyriology, the ignorance of which disciplines was a major critique Loisy levelled against Renan.[16] His Assyriological work exposed him to a comparative historical approach, which has dominated the fields of ancient Near Eastern studies more so than the more literary historical-critical approach (e.g., source criticism),[17] which has typified much of nineteenth- through twenty-first-century biblical scholarship.[18] Loisy's work in biblical studies, however, aided his mastery of this historical critical approach, which in his day was epitomized in the work of mainly German biblical scholars like Julius Wellhausen (1844–1918).

In his own biblical scholarship, Loisy combined both approaches. Whereas nineteenth-century historical critics like Wellhausen tended to ignore Assyriological findings (despite Wellhausen's competence in Assyriology including knowledge of Akkadian),[19] Loisy frequently engaged Assyriological texts, some of which he translated himself. In regard to Loisy's broad training in biblical studies and ancillary fields Charles Talar notes that, "The cumulative effect of these studies was to expose the gulf that existed between the traditional teaching of the Church and the intellectual

---

15. Loisy, *Choses passées*, 66. Unless otherwise mentioned, all English translations are my own.

16. On Loisy's studies and scholarship in Assyriology see, e.g., Morrow, *Alfred Loisy*; and earlier Morrow, "Babylon in Paris," 261–76.

17. On the early lack of such historical critical (primarily literary) approach to studying ancient Near Eastern literature at that time, and well into the twentieth-century, see, e.g., Hallo, "Limits of Skepticism," 187–99; and Hallo, "New Viewpoints," 13–26. It might be true to say developing a literary historical critical method in ancient Near Eastern studies is only really beginning now in the twenty-first century, and with such texts Loisy himself examined, regarding Mesopotamian flood traditions, e.g., Chen, *Primeval Flood*.

18. On the dominance of source criticism in biblical studies, especially Pentateuchal studies, see, e.g., Bergsma and Morrow, *Murmuring Against Moses*.

19. See Machinist, "Road Not Taken," 469–531.

milieu of modernity. And to instill in Loisy the conviction that a work of revisionism was necessary to close that gap."[20]

Early on, as he taught at the Institut catholique, Loisy commenced his lectures on Scripture with matters concerning the history of the canonization process of Scripture, as well as the various issues concerning textual criticism and the transmission of the various biblical manuscripts in different languages. His earliest publications in Scripture emerged from these lectures. That became his typical *modus operandi*; first he would lecture on a topic, then that would form the basis of his journal articles (which were not mere copies of his lectures), which he would then republish in book form. He only later moved to more controversial matters like those concerning source criticism of the Pentateuch or other areas of historical critical scholarship. The year before Leo XIII's *Providentissimus Deus*, and Loisy's dismissal from the Institut catholique, marked the beginning of his scholarly article publications in *L'enseignement biblique*,[21] which was a periodical he founded in hopes of making his scholarship more available to priests after they graduated from seminary but who were looking for accessible information on Scripture.

Loisy's Early Biblical Work

Loisy's earliest works in biblical studies pertained to the history of the canonization process of Scripture. He would turn to the study of textual criticism, and then begin his published forays into source criticism by examining the Wisdom literature of the Old Testament. The period under discussion in this present chapter cover a mere three years, and yet Loisy was an incredibly productive scholar during this short time; he published eight books and thirty scholarly journal articles.

---

20. Talar, "Between Science," 28.
21. Most of the material he published in *L'enseignement biblique* was republished in book volumes, but I have been unable to access any of the editions of *L'enseignement biblique* in order to check how closely they were to the book forms.

Histories of the Biblical Canon: Loisy's Entry into Biblical Scholarship

Loisy's entry into biblical scholarship was his work on the history of the Old Testament canon, *Histoire du Canon de l'Ancien Testament*.[22] This 259-page volume originated in lectures he gave as professor of Sacred Scripture at the Institut catholique de Paris from 1889–1890. This was a wide-ranging volume that covers an immense amount of time, dealing both with Christian and Jewish traditions and history. This was primarily a work of church history wherein he took readers from the earliest centuries through the period of the Reformation. In addition to important scholarly sources like Richard Simon (1638–1712), Johann Salomo Semler (1725–1791), Johann Gottfried Eichhorn (1752–1827), and Édouard Guillaume Eugène Reuss (1804–1891), Loisy included thoughtful discussions of material culled widely from the church fathers (East and West) and from Jewish sources like the Talmud.

At the outset of the volume, Loisy described the study of Scripture, the way it is typically taught, as, "a very dry subject."[23] He proceeded to examine the history of the canonization process for the Old Testament but began with internal evidence from the Old Testament itself. Most of the volume dealt with the history of the Christian canon of the Old Testament, by which he meant the deuterocanonical books: 1 and 2 Maccabees; Judith; Tobit; Wisdom of Solomon; Sirach; and Baruch. He displayed quite an impressive command of the historical evidence from the church fathers, the medieval period, the renaissance, the Protestant Reformers themselves, as well as from the Enlightenment and nineteenth century. But what was perhaps most important in relation to his later work and the question of the role of historical criticism in biblical studies, was the first roughly sixty pages where he explored questions concerning the Old Testament canon prior to Christianity.

Loisy noted that Édouard Reuss denied the Pentateuch was in its final form by the time of Nehemiah. Loisy proceeded to modify

---

22. Loisy, *Histoire du Canon*.
23. Loisy, *Histoire du Canon*, 1.

Reuss's comment in a very nuanced way. In doing this, however, Loisy added heft to Reuss's claim by pointing out that the books of Maccabees never mentioned the Torah, nor did they display any evidence they were aware of the Torah.[24] His conclusion, was that, "the origin of the canon coincides with the redaction and the first promulgation of the Law. In fact, the Law becomes fully and forever canonical by the official promulgation of it by Ezra."[25] This would be a controversial claim in the Catholic world of Loisy's day.

The following year Loisy published a companion volume on the history of the New Testament canonization process, *Histoire du Canon du Nouveau Testament*.[26] As with the prior book, this volume also originated from his lectures at the Institut catholique[27] from 1890–1891. Slightly larger than his prior volume, at 305 pages, he also included citations of scholarship from a wider range of languages, this time including English, e.g., J. B. Lightfoot (1828–1889) and B. F. Westcott (1825–1901).[28] His volume began by the discussing the Old Testament as an important inheritance from the Jewish people via Jesus' apostles.[29] These comments prepared for his transition from the prior volume's focus on the Old Testament, to this volume's discussion of the New Testament canon. His book covered an incredible amount of material, walking through the early formation of the New Testament canon,[30] the various discussions and examples of New Testament canons from the fourth and fifth centuries all the way through the Council of Trent,[31] and

---

24. Loisy, *Histoire du Canon*, 46. This last point is not that different from the recent argument made in Collins, *Invention of Judaism*.

25. Loisy, *Histoire du Canon*, 53.

26. Loisy, *Histoire du Canon NT*.

27. In the book, Loisy referred to the Institut catholique as L'École supérieure de théologie de Paris.

28. Other scholars upon whom he relied include Simon, Louis Duchesne, Ferdinand Christian Baur (1792–1860), David Friedrich Strauss (1808–1874), Reuss, Theodor Zahn (1838–1933), Harnack, and Renan.

29. Loisy, *Histoire du Canon NT*, 1.

30. Loisy, *Histoire du Canon NT*, 3–138.

31. Loisy, *Histoire du Canon NT*, 139–233.

it concludes with Trent's discussion and definition of the canon as well as the discussion after Trent.[32]

Early on Loisy brought to the attention of readers that the study of church history, and in particular the historical of biblical canonization, demonstrated that there was a sort of deuterocanon of the New Testament; there were a number of books (2 Peter, 2 and 3 John, Hebrews, James, Jude, and Revelation) that were not used by Christians everywhere, were more contested than the others, and only became universally accepted over a period of time culminating by the very end of the fourth century.[33] Loisy included in this context mention of particular texts in the Gospels (Mark 16:9-20; Luke 22:43-44; and John 7:53—8:11) that appeared to him as deuterocanonical, since they were not evident in all of the manuscript tradition. His history made it clear that the limits of the New Testament canon were ambiguous in the earliest centuries; a number of texts, like the Shepherd of Hermas, which were later excluded were considered part of the New Testament in some Christian communities.

Loisy's work spanned more than a millennium-and-a-half of Christian history. He included a helpful discussion of Gnosticism and Gnostic sources in their uses of the New Testament.[34] He also detailed the important role of Marcion in the earliest debates about the canon.[35] When it came to the important decisions of the fourth and fifth centuries, Loisy explained the prominence of the Bible in Africa, and particularly the key synods of Hippo (393) and the Third Synod of Carthage (397).[36] He treated extensively Eusebius' discussion,[37] and had a lot to say later about the Protestant Reformers, although here he relied primarily upon Reuss' French translations of their works, probably because that was more readily

---

32. Loisy, *Histoire du Canon NT*, 235-302.
33. Loisy, *Histoire du Canon NT*, 6.
34. Loisy, *Histoire du Canon NT*, 64-69.
35. Loisy, *Histoire du Canon NT*, 69-77.
36. Loisy, *Histoire du Canon NT*, 107-11.
37. Loisy, *Histoire du Canon NT*, 151-63.

available to him, since he was certainly more than competent to read their German and Latin works.

If, in his consideration of the Old Testament canon, the controversial area Loisy brought up that best prepared for his later work in historical criticism pertained to the origin of the Pentateuch, then in this volume the comparable discussion is on the question of Matthean priority. Historically, until rather late in the nineteenth-century, the universal tradition within Christianity and among scholars was that Matthew's Gospel was the first written. That began to be challenged in the nineteenth-century, especially by the work of Heinrich Julius Holtzmann (1832–1910), Loisy's contemporary.[38] In other works Loisy followed Holtzmann in arguing for the priority of the Gospel of Mark, which would become the dominant position among English and German speaking scholars in the twentieth century and today in the twenty first century. In this volume, Loisy spent special time focusing on the witness of Papias, as preserved in Eusebius, and challenging their testimony on Matthean priority, although without arguing for Markan priority.[39]

Loisy raised doubts about other matters as well, all of which he grounded in the historical debates within the Christian tradition. These included doubts about the apostle John's authorship of 2 and 3 John,[40] the Pauline authorship of Hebrews,[41] and, perhaps most importantly, the link between the Council of Trent's apparent attribution of authorship of biblical texts and the possibility of faithful Catholic questioning such attributions.[42] This last point is significant because he went back into questions about traditional

---

38. On the importance of Holtzmann here within his historical and political context, see, e.g., Hahn and Morrow, *Modern Biblical Criticism*, 212–17.

39. Although he did not argue here for Markan priority, he did discuss the issue of a Proto-Matthew and Proto-Mark. See Loisy, *Histoire du Canon NT*, 39n1.

40. Loisy, *Histoire du Canon NT*, 194 and 202.

41. Loisy, *Histoire du Canon NT*, 205–6.

42. E.g., Loisy, *Histoire du Canon NT*, 256–57.

attributions of authorship for Old Testament books, even though his focus in this volume was on the New Testament.

Loisy began with Proverbs, which eventually would be his first topic of study that got him directly involved in historical biblical criticism. Loisy explained, "This is the case of Proverbs, which could not be attributed to Solomon in their entirety, and of Wisdom, which cannot be attributed to him at all."[43] Immediately following this, he continued: "Here, the modern notion of authenticity has almost no application, unless we call these books authentic for the simple reason that they exist and that the tradition recommends them."[44]

Loisy attempted to provide evidence that attributions of authorship, even by a council such as Trent, did not mean that every portion of the book had to be attributed to that author. How could it when the Proverbs of Solomon identifies others as responsible for portions of its collection? In a footnote he likewise quotes a lengthy Latin passage from a traditional source, none other than St. Robert Bellarmine (1542–1621), which Loisy interpreted as implying the Pentateuch's final form came at the time of Ezra, long after Moses.[45] Thus Loisy argued that the common understanding of the Mosaic authorship of the Pentateuch be "interpreted in a relatively broad sense."[46] Loisy explained why he did not think that

43. Loisy, *Histoire du Canon NT*, 256.
44. Loisy, *Histoire du Canon NT*.
45. Loisy, *Histoire du Canon NT*, 256–57n1. Bellarmine's Latin is a bit more ambiguous, only attributing the last portion concerning Moses' death to Ezra, his relationship with the rest of the Pentateuch is less clear here: "Until the time of Ezra, the Scriptures had not been reduced to the form of books, so that they could be easily and conveniently possessed, but were scattered in various annals and papers, and sometimes through negligence of the priests they were not found for a long time, as is clear from 2 Kings 22, where it is related as something new that in the days of Josiah a single volume of the Law of the Lord was found in the temple. But Ezra, after the captivity, collected them all and reduced them together into one body, adding to Deuteronomy the last chapter on the life of Moses, and some others here and there to continue the history." This is my own translation of the Latin quotation that Loisy included in his volume.
46. Loisy, *Histoire du Canon NT*, 256.

the Council's use of the name Moses as the Pentateuch's author required the belief that the Pentateuch's final form, with any and all redactions, etc., must be understood as coming from Moses.

Textual Criticism and Bible Versions

From dealing with the biblical canon, Loisy moved to textual criticism and the study of the biblical manuscript tradition, including the various early translations. Both volumes he published on this topic were part of the same work, titled *Histoire critique du texte et des versions de la Bible*. The first volume dealt with the text of the Old Testament,[47] and the second volume dealt with the versions in their various translations.[48] The first volume, *Histoire critique du texte de l'Ancien Testament*, spanned 314 pages, most of which were initially published in his periodical *L'enseignement biblique*. Despite his initial intent with that periodical, serving parish priests, this work was clearly intended for scholars who knew Hebrew and the relevant languages. As such, he cited a plethora of early modern, Enlightenment, and contemporary scholars on a host of related issues, in their relevant primary languages,[49] including the English work of Solomon Schechter (1847–1915) the father of Conservative Judaism in the U.S.

Roughly the first hundred pages of this volume covered the history of the Hebrew language in the context of other ancient languages. Loisy wrote magisterially, and this is not without

---

47. Loisy, *Histoire critique du texte I.I.*
48. Loisy, *Histoire critique du texte I.II.*
49. These included Simon, Johann Gottfried Eichhorn (1752–1827), Antoine Isaac Baron Silvestre de Sacy (1758–1838), Wilhelm Martin Leberecht de Wette (1780–1849), Heinrich Friedrich Wilhelm Gesenius (1786–1842), Karl Heinrich Graf (1815–1869), Georg Heinrich August Ewald (1803–1875), Austen Henry Layard (1817–1894), Vigouroux, Renan, François Lenormant (1837–1883), Paul de Lagarde (1827–1891), F. Max Müller (1823–1900), Eberhard Schrader (1836–1908), Samuel Rolles Driver (1846–1914), Gaston Camille Charles Maspero (1846–1916), Joseph Halévy (1827–1917), Friedrich Delitzsch (1850–1922), Archibald Sayce (1845–1933), Sir William Matthew Flinders Petrie (1853–1942), Wellhausen, and Theodor Nöldeke (1836–1930).

reason. Some of his teachers, Renan, Joseph Halévy (1827–1917), and Jules Oppert (1825–1905), were internationally renowned philologists covering a wide range of ancient languages.[50] He covered a variety of textual critical matters throughout the remainder of the volume, including covering important principles of textual criticism.[51] Near the end of the volume, he concluded with the importance of textual criticism, which he wanted to underscore, namely, "But textual criticism, it cannot be repeated too often, has its reason for being since the text of the Bible has not reached us without alteration."[52]

At 245 pages, Loisy's second volume, *Histoire critique des versions de l'Ancien Testament*, was shorter than his first volume, but it too originated in articles published in *L'enseignement biblique*. In this book, Loisy looked at many of the ancient versions of the Old Testament in the many languages into which it was translated. Most of the volume was devoted to the history[53] and textual criticism[54] of the Septuagint Greek translation, although he covered other Greek translations as well. Throughout the rest of the volume, he discussed other Greek editions coming from Hebrew,[55] Coptic editions,[56] Ethiopian versions,[57] Armenian translations,[58] the Old Testament in Syriac,[59] Arabic texts of the Old Testament,[60] and Gothic editions.[61]

---

50. Oppert and Halévy served as readers for Loisy's Assyriology thesis on the royal annals of Sargon II. See, e.g., Morrow, *Alfred Loisy*; and Morrow, "Babylon in Paris," 261–76.

51. Loisy, *Histoire critique du texte I.I.*, 203–50.

52. Loisy, *Histoire critique du texte I.I.*, 308.

53. Loisy, *Histoire critique du texte I.II.*, 3–81.

54. Loisy, *Histoire critique du texte I.II.*, 82–163.

55. Loisy, *Histoire critique du texte I.II.*, 164–219.

56. Loisy, *Histoire critique du texte I.II.*, 220–29.

57. Loisy, *Histoire critique du texte I.II.*, 229–31.

58. Loisy, *Histoire critique du texte I.II.*, 232–34.

59. Loisy, *Histoire critique du texte I.II.*, 234–38.

60. Loisy, *Histoire critique du texte I.II.*, 238–40.

61. Loisy, *Histoire critique du texte I.II.*, 240–41.

Wisdom Literature: Loisy's Starting Point for Source Criticism

Loisy's published works in historical biblical criticism really began with his forays into the Old Testament Wisdom literature, first with Proverbs, and then with the Book of Job. He initially published three articles on Proverbs in 1890 in the journal *Revue des Religions*,[62] which eventually formed his book length study. The book version, *Les Proverbes de Salomon*,[63] was published the same year. It was incredibly short, a mere 59 pages; more of a booklet really. Unlike his scholarly tomes on textual criticism, this slender volume was unencumbered by numerous scholarly references, although he did make some references to scholars.[64] He remarked how unique the Old Testament Wisdom literature is; it is more abstract and philosophical than the rest of the Hebrew texts of the Old Testament.[65] After his introductory comments, Loisy was able to turn to historical critical matters.

He explained how the original text of Proverbs appeared to have been modified through oral transmission, or else in the process of scribal transmission.[66] Mentioning the subheadings found throughout Proverbs, Loisy asserted that they had no historical or chronological value in helping dating the text or its redaction.[67] He recognized that the ancient interpreters, in both the Jewish and Christian traditions, understood Solomon to be the author of the complete text of Proverbs, but Loisy pointed out that the text itself appeared to imply it had other authors as well. This is where Loisy was able to bring up contemporary debates about the authorship of biblical documents, and he used the opportunity

---

62. Loisy, "Les Proverbes I," 28–44; Loisy, "Les Proverbes II," 97–115; and Loisy, "Les Proverbes III," 217–40. The first article became the first seventeen pages of his book, the second article became the next roughly eighteen pages, and the third article formed the remaining twenty-three pages of the book.

63. Loisy, *Les Proverbes*.

64. E.g., Eichhorn, de Wette, Reuss, and Ewald.

65. Loisy, *Les Proverbes*, 1.

66. Loisy, *Les Proverbes*, 9.

67. Loisy, *Les Proverbes*, 12.

to point out that even "conservative" exegetes recognized that Proverbs assumed other authors.[68]

Loisy was able to soften the blow of his source critical comments, not only by pointing out that the text of Proverbs implies as much, but also in juxtaposing the more radical ideas of Reuss. He linked Reuss with "La nouvelle école rationaliste" ("the new rationalist school") and he brought up Reuss's notion that Proverbs might include vestigial traces of polygamy and polytheism, from which Loisy distanced himself.[69] In the end, Loisy thought the date of the composition and final redaction of Proverbs was uncertain,[70] but the entire discussion of attributing Proverbs to multiple sources helped pave the way for further work in source criticism, introducing this method more widely into Catholic discussions.

From Proverbs, Loisy turned to the Book of Job with his 175 page 1892 *Le Livre de Job*.[71] As with many of his other works covered thus far, *Le Livre de Job* began as (two) installments in *L'enseignement biblique*. Loisy showed in this volume that he was clearly knowledgeable in both Masoretic and Septuagint textual traditions, as well as the Vulgate, to all of which he made references throughout. The first eighty-seven pages represent his introduction to Job, and the remainder were his translation of the text, with helpful footnotes explaining his translation, or some point concerning the text, the manuscript tradition, or other scholarly renditions of a word.

Loisy not only brought his biblical scholarship to bear on the text, but also engaged the tradition, most notably Gregory the Great's famous allegorical commentary *Moralia in Iob* and Thomas Aquinas' commentary. He contrasted the two, showing a preference for Aquinas, explaining that while Gregory the Great commented on Job allegorically, "the Angelic Doctor himself inaugurates another method of exegesis, by seeking principally the

68. Loisy, *Les Proverbes*, 18.
69. Loisy, *Les Proverbes*, 19.
70. Loisy, *Les Proverbes*, 33.
71. Loisy, *Le Livre de Job*.

literal sense."[72] At the same time, Loisy explicitly contested Aquinas' claims in his commentary where Aquinas affirmed that Job's real historical existence was very important for the truth of the Book of Job's content, namely of what the biblical book taught. In contrast, Loisy responded, "The author of Job is not a historian, he is a moralist. The truth of the story he sets forth consists in a just proportion to the lesson he wishes to draw from it, not in an exact relationship with real facts."[73] Rhetorically, Loisy was able to use some of his sources to help the cause of source criticism. In the context of discussing questions of authorship, where even the tradition was not unanimous, Loisy employed his own former teacher Vigouroux, known as a conservative apologist, arguing for a similar point regarding the biblical Psalms.[74]

Assyriology and Biblical Studies

Loisy published a wide variety of works in Assyriology throughout his career, particularly prior to his 1908 excommunication. In the period under discussion in this present volume, the most important of his works was his book applying Assyriology to the creation and flood accounts in the book of Genesis, *Les mythes chaldéens de la création et du Déluge*,[75] although the majority of the volume focused on the Akkadian accounts in their own right, without reference to the Bible. Throughout this book, Loisy introduced the language of "mythe" (myth), "légende" (legend), and related words to describe the Mesopotamian accounts he would utilize to compare with the biblical accounts in Genesis.[76]

72. Loisy, *Le Livre de Job*, 4.
73. Loisy, *Le Livre de Job*, 45.
74. Loisy, *Le Livre de Job*, 40n1.
75. Loisy, *Les mythes chaldéens*.
76. In this volume, Loisy employed "mythe" and "légende" almost synonymously, which contrasts greatly with how he later distinguished these words as a secular scholar of the history of religion at the Collège de France from 1909 and on, after his correspondence with the Belgian scholar Franz Cumont (1868–1947). In *Les mythes chaldéens* Loisy employed one or the other word

In the very first line Loisy wrote in this volume he defined "myth" as follows: "Myths are the dogmas of pagan religions, floating dogmas, poorly defined, in the formation of which imagination plays a greater part than reasoning or, at least, than sound reason."[77] Although he was not completely consistent with this definition in this volume, he tended to use "myth" to refer to a story, whether whole or fragmentary. In general, at this point, he was careful to avoid applying the term "myth" to the Bible, reserving it for exclusively for the Akkadian accounts.[78] The bulk of *Les mythes chaldéens* focused on the Akkadian creation account *Enuma Elish*.[79] After this, he included a lengthy discussion of the Akkadian flood narrative the *Epic of Gilgamesh*.[80] He reserved his discussion of parallels with the biblical accounts to the end of the volume.[81] His conclusions were important for combining source-critical discussions, using classical Wellhausenian sources, with a comparative Assyriological approach. He argued that most likely the various documentary sources worked with available Babylonian traditions.[82]

Études Bibliques

The last volume I will consider here in this chapter was published just after the time period covered, but it included four chapters originally published between 1892 and 1893, and thus I conclude with Loisy's important *Études bibliques*.[83] At the outset, in his

---

(singular or plural) thirty-seven times.

77. Loisy, *Les mythes chaldéens*, 1.

78. In his later work, Loisy, *Les mythes babyloniens*, he would occasionally apply «légende» to the biblical accounts, but even then he reserved such terms primarily for non-biblical ancient Near Eastern accounts.

79. Loisy, *Les mythes chaldéens*, 2–39.

80. Loisy, *Les mythes chaldéens*, 39–81.

81. Loisy, *Les mythes chaldéens*, 82–95.

82. Loisy, *Les mythes chaldéens*, 93.

83. Loisy's Études *bibliques* went through three editions during his life. The first was published in 1894, the second in 1901, and the third in 1903. I was

unpaginated Avant-propos, Loisy explained his purpose in collecting together these articles into one volume, namely, "the reconciliation of Catholic dogma and discipline with the scientific study of the Bible."[84] His first essay in the second edition of *Études bibliques* was his chapter titled, "Biblical Criticism."[85] The content of this essay Loisy delivered as his inaugural lecture on Scripture for the academic year 1892–1893, which he first published in *L'enseignement biblique*.

In this first essay, Loisy mentioned that he found hardly any evidence of scholarly biblical criticism prior to the seventeenth century works of figures like Louis Cappel (1585–1658) and Richard Simon.[86] Here Loisy laid out how he defined "criticism": "The word criticism means judgment, discernment, examination, the art of judging. Criticism is now understood to mean the reasoned examination of the works of the human mind. Criticism is an art rather than a science."[87] More precisely, regarding the application of "criticism" to texts, Loisy wrote: "Applied to texts, criticism is concerned with verifying the integrity of their conservation, their origin, their meaning, and with appreciating their character."[88] He proceeded to discuss the importance of textual criticism,[89] all the while maintaining that in some sense, "Without a doubt, as a divine book, the Bible is above criticism,"

---

unable to access the original 1894 edition, and here I rely upon the second edition, Loisy, *Études bibliques*. The original 1894 edition was only about 91 pages, and the second edition was 161 pages. The first chapter from the first edition was removed in the second edition, and the final two chapters in the second addition were added from articles Loisy published in *Revue du clergé français*, which will not be covered here.

84. Loisy, *Études bibliques*, n.p.

85. Loisy, *Études bibliques*, 7–25.

86. Loisy, *Études bibliques*, 7.

87. Loisy, *Études bibliques*, 8. Writing further on the same page, he elaborated, "It presupposes not only sufficient knowledge of the subject to which it applies, but experience of the things which are to be judged, and, if one may express it thus, the handling of the objects which are to be appreciated in themselves and compared with each other."

88. Loisy, *Études bibliques*, 8.

89. Loisy, *Études bibliques*, 9.

but, he points out, it is also "a human book."[90] Thus, in light of the fact that the Bible is "a human book," in addition to being "a divine book," Loisy concluded, "We must comment on the Bible with all the exactness that is now brought to the examination of documents from profane antiquity."[91]

The next two essays, "The History of Dogma and Inspiration"[92] and "The Biblical Question and the Inspiration of Scripture,"[93] dealt with the issue of biblical inspiration. The focus of the first was on the French Assyriologist François Lenormant's views concerning biblical inspiration, which were very close to Loisy's own notions: "Everything is inspired, not everything is revealed."[94] The second one dealt with Maurice d'Hulst and "la question biblique" (the biblical question), which precipitated Pope Leo XIII's promulgation of *Providentissimus Deus*. Loisy's conclusion supported the importance of serious Catholic engagement in historical biblical criticism. He wrote, "The peril at the present hour is not to advance on the path of science; it would be to remain immobile, denying the movement that has been accomplished and is still being accomplished around us."[95] His final 1893 essay included in this volume, "The Eleven First Chapters of Genesis,"[96] was primarily a response to an English language attempt at reconciling Genesis with Assyriological findings. Loisy brought his Assyriological expertise to bear in response to the author.

---

90. Loisy, *Études bibliques*, 11.
91. Loisy, *Études bibliques*, 23.
92. Loisy, *Études bibliques*, 26–37.
93. Loisy, *Études bibliques*, 38–60.
94. Lenormant, *Les origines*, xvi. Later, Loisy mentioned in passing the difficulty of reconciling biblical criticism with "the theory of the absolute inerrancy of Scripture." See Loisy, *Études bibliques*, 50.
95. Loisy, *Études bibliques*, 48.
96. Loisy, *Études bibliques*, 61–78.

Conclusion: An Important Part of the History Leading to Vatican II and Beyond

Loisy made his goal clear early on: "Everywhere I have wanted to reconcile the tradition and healthy criticism, to join the prudence of the theologian to the sincerity of the scholar, without sacrificing one to the other."[97] This is a worthy goal whether or not Loisy achieved it. One of the important points Loisy brought up, in the context of his work on the Wisdom literature, was to emphasize how, "The Scriptures were written in accordance with the literary customs of antiquity."[98] This sounds a lot like what the Second Vatican Council would later teach in its Dogmatic Constitution on Divine Revelation, *Dei Verbum*. In similar fashion to how *Dei Verbum* no. 12 would emphasize the study of the history, languages, customs, manner of speech, etc., of the broader cultural context in which the Bible was written, for proper biblical interpretation, so too, Loisy wrote more than seventy years earlier:

> Then comes the interpretation of the document whose content and provenance have been established. In this part of its task, criticism has as indispensable auxiliaries the knowledge of languages, history, and institutions of antiquity; without which the exegesis of ancient documents will be full of misinterpretations. To explain these documents accurately, it is necessary to enter completely into the spirit of antiquity, not to thoughtlessly attribute to the ancients our ways of seeing, reasoning, and feeling; it is necessary to make oneself provisionally a citizen of past centuries.[99]

Loisy's early works of biblical scholarship charted the course he would travel until his excommunication in 1908. Prior to this, he attempted to bring the full measure of contemporary nineteenth-century trends in historical biblical criticism and comparative ancient Near Eastern scholarship into the realm of

---

97. Loisy, *Histoire du Canon de l'Ancien Testament*, 2.
98. Loisy, *Le Livre de Job*, 35.
99. Loisy, *Études bibliques*, 10.

Catholic exegesis. In one autobiographical reflection, in reference to his critique of Harnack, Loisy explains what he was after: "I was discreetly but truly insinuating an essential reform of biblical exegesis, of all theology, and even of Catholicism in general."[100] In the next chapter, the final chapter in this book, I will look at some ways in which Loisy anticipated Vatican II in his ecclesiological discussion in *L'Évangile et l'Église*.

---

100. Loisy, *Choses passées*, 246.

5

Loisy on the Way to Vatican II

Introduction

IN THE FIRST CHAPTER of *Lumen Gentium*, we read the following: "Christ, therefore, in order to fulfil the will of the Father, inaugurated the kingdom of heaven on earth and revealed to us its mystery... The Church, as the kingdom of Christ already present in mystery, by the power of God in the world, visibly grows" (no. 3).[1] For much of Christian history, the kingdom of God was viewed as present now, but not yet present in its fullness, which awaits the *eschaton*, the final end of all things. *Nunc et tunc*: now and then, at that time.[2] Certainly one aspect of Loisy's *L'Évangile et l'Église* that

---

1. Latin text taken from Tanner, ed., *Decrees II*, p. 850. Throughout this chapter, unless otherwise noted, all English translations are my own.

2. For this discussion of the history of theological reflection on the kingdom of God, and its relation to the Church, I am indebted to Schönborn, "Kingdom of God," 217–34, especially his subsection, "The Church and the Kingdom of God," 222–23. One of the main points of Schönborn's article is to demonstrate, especially in light of *Lumen Gentium*, that "the Church is the kingdom" (232) of God, or as he writes earlier, "there lies no distance between the Church

is difficult to miss is the eschatological character of the kingdom of God.[3] Loisy famously wrote, in what many have taken to be an apparent judgment against the Church, "Jesus announced the kingdom, and it is the Church that came."[4] Even Joseph Ratzinger noted that Loisy's intent, in context, was not to create so wide a gap between the kingdom and the Church that the two have no relation to one another, as to be completely disparate.[5] Neverthe-

---

and the kingdom of God . . . The *pilgrim* Church is the kingdom . . . but the Church in the glory of heaven is the perfected kingdom . . ." (226). In this article, Schönborn "withdraw[s]" his prior identification of the "the Church as the sacrament of the kingdom," which he had thought was the teaching of *Lumen Gentium*, and which he has seen taught by other theologians. He is here attempting to correct this notion, which he finds nowhere in the documents of the Second Vatican Council (223–24 and 224 n. 23). The earlier view that Schönborn withdraws he published in Schönborn, "Il significativo," 23.

3. Unless otherwise mentioned, all citations from *L'Évangile et l'Église* will be taken from the expanded 2nd ed., Loisy, *L'Évangile et l'Église*. This version adds, at the beginning, an additional chapter, devoted to the sources of the Gospels. An English translation is available online as Loisy, *Gospel and the Church*. On Loisy's "apocalyptic" Jesus in *L'Évangile et l'Église*, see Dietrich, "Loisy," 303–11. When citing from *L'Évangile et l'Église* in what follows I first cite from the French edition placing the English translation (ET) page number in parentheses.

4. Loisy, *L'Évangile et l'Église*, 155 (ET, 166). Schönborn has even written, "The secularization of the idea of the kingdom of God is one of the possible consequences of the radical eschatologism that has dominated the discussions about the relationship between the Church and the kingdom of God since Johannes Weiss, Alfred Loisy, and Albert Schweitzer." See Schönborn, "Kingdom of God," 227. He traces the genealogy back to Hermann Samuel Reimarus, through Eduard Reuss, and then popularized by Loisy's own teacher Ernest Renan (228–29). Schönborn is here following the arguments of Carmignac, *Le mirage*, which he considers to be "a very important book" (227n28).

5. Ratzinger, *Called to Communion*, 21n6, "I myself probably contributed to its spread by treating it in my lessons and by adopting it from Peterson and Schlier, though in a substantially modified form, in my article 'Kirche' in *LThK* [*Lexikon für Theologie und Kirche*]. Unfortunately, these alterations have been wiped away in the process of popularization; the maxim was lined with an interpretation that found no support even in Loisy's original meaning." He omits this nuance in Ratzinger/Benedict XVI, *Jesus of Nazareth I*, 48, when he writes, "Another variant of this alleged gulf between Jesus and the preaching of the Apostles occurs in the now famous saying of the Catholic modernist Alfred Loisy, who put it like this: Jesus preached the Kingdom of God, and

less, in the conclusion to his work on modernism, Marie-Joseph Lagrange quipped, in partial response to Loisy, "The kingdom of God has come, it is the Church."[6]

In the last chapter, we took a look at Loisy's early work in Scripture, prior to his excommunication, and mostly before 1893 and his forced resignation from the Institut catholique. In this final chapter I examine *L'Évangile et l'Église* specifically as regards Loisy's ecclesiology.[7] After some initial comments on context, I discuss some of the ecclesiological points Loisy's work raised, especially regarding the relationship of the kingdom of God to the Church. In some ways, which I shall highlight, Loisy's work anticipated the work of the Second Vatican Council in its Dogmatic Constitution on the Church, *Lumen Gentium*. His de-emphasis on the present aspect of the kingdom of God in favor of a more distant kingdom of God coming in the future, in *L'Évangile et l'Église*, would contrast with *Lumen Gentium*, which envisioned the kingdom as "already present in mystery" (no. 3). Nevertheless, other ideas present in Loisy's work, like those on the laity, would fit well what *Lumen Gentium* includes in chapters 4 and 5 on the laity and the universal call to holiness respectively.

L'Évangile et l'Église in Context

Marvin O'Connell has called *L'Évangile et l'Église* "the most important work of his [Loisy's] life."[8] This is but one reason for another examination of Loisy's classic work. Moreover, *L'Évangile et l'Église*, along with his later expanded discussion and defense in *Autour d'un petit livre*, contains what might be the most sustained ecclesiological comments that he published.[9] Many have identified

---

what came was the Church. These words may be considered ironic, but they also express sadness."

6. Lagrange, *M. Loisy*, 244.

7. For helpful discussions of *L'Évangile et l'Église* situating it in its context, see Geyer, *Wahrheit*; and Hill, "Loisy's *L'Évangile*," 73–98.

8. O'Connell, *Critics on Trial*, 241.

9. See Loisy, *Autour*, 157–86, in his, "Letter to a Catholic Apologist: On the

this slender volume as the matchstick that ignited the controversy over modernism.¹⁰ This book thus forms part of the context of Loisy's excommunication six years after its initial publication.¹¹ What complicates matters, however, is that *L'Évangile et l'Église* is notoriously difficult to interpret.¹² Loisy writes with what Charles Talar has called a "studied ambiguity."¹³ Moreover, although Loisy wrote many autobiographical narratives detailing the background to his work, these autobiographies themselves remain difficult to interpret.¹⁴ To what degree are Loisy's later reflections accurate windows into his mind prior to his excommunication? To what extent did Loisy's excommunication and additional apologetical motivations affect his retelling of his own history prior to his excommunication? These are difficult questions to answer.

As studies of Loisy have continued to pour forth, it becomes increasingly apparent that Loisy's motivations for publishing *L'Évangile et l'Église*, were manifold. Clearly in part he was responding to Adolf Harnack's *Das Wesen des Christentums* initially published two years earlier, which is explicitly what his book states as his motivation.¹⁵ It appears further that perhaps part of the motive, however small a part, for publishing *L'Évangile et l'Église* stemmed from concern about the see of Monaco.¹⁶ Prince Albert

---

Foundation and the Authority of the Church."

10. Ward De Pril sees the "origins of the conflict" that led to the Modernist controversy in Loisy's teachers Ernest Renan and Louis Duchesne. See De Pril, "Modernism," 377–96.

11. On the background surrounding the Holy See's investigations of Loisy, the placing of some of his books on the *Index*, and his 1908 excommunication, see Arnold, "Roman Magisterium," 159–69; and Arnold and Losito, ed., *La censure*.

12. Hill, "Loisy's *L'Évangile*," 73; Talar, *Metaphor and Modernist*, 107–8 and 164–65; Daly, *Transcendence and Immanence*, 55–58; and Poulat, *Histoire, dogme, et critique*, 90–92.

13. Talar, *Metaphor and Modernist*, 107. See also Daly, "Theological and Philosophical," 106.

14. Hill, "More than a Biblical Critic," 689–707; and Talar, *(Re)reading*, 165–90.

15. All citations will be taken from Harnack, *Das Wesen*.

16. Hill, "Loisy's *L'Évangile*," 88–89; Hill, "French Politics," 526; O'Connell,

of Monaco submitted Loisy's name as one of his candidates for bishop, and Loisy strongly desired the appointment. Perhaps such a thoroughgoing apologetic against Harnack would win him favor in the eyes of at least some members of the Catholic hierarchy. And of course, as *L'Évangile et l'Église* originated from his unpublished *Essais d'histoire et de philosophie religieuses*, this would be one means of seeing into print a portion of that more controversial work that was so dear to his heart.[17] All of these pieces complicate the matter of the text's interpretation. Moreover, as is clear from Loisy's own autobiographical statements in private letters and in published form, he intended *L'Évangile et l'Église* to serve as part of his program of reform, of the transformation of Catholicism from within. As he explained in *Choses passées*: "Therefore I did not limit myself to criticizing M. Harnack, I implied discreetly but really an essential reform of biblical exegesis, of the entirety of theology, and even of Catholicism in general."[18]

Talar similarly observes that Loisy's attack was broader than simply a critique of Harnack: "Loisy's challenge to the prevailing system [within Catholicism] took the proximate form of a subversion of Harnack's book on Christianity's essence."[19] Furthermore, "In critiquing Harnack's work from his perspective as historian, Loisy was able to 'defamiliarize' the essentialist norms of neoscholasticism, juxtaposing them with 'the facts' in order to point up the need for their revision."[20] Considering his context, Loisy's subtlety is understandable.

Critics on Trial, 236–51; and O'Connell, "Bishopric of Monaco," 26–51.

17. As Hill notes, "internal evidence reinforces the impression that *L'Évangile et l'Église* was at least partly Loisy's effort to publish the ideas of the 'Essais' using Harnack's new book as the occasion." See Hill, "Loisy's *L'Évangile*," 78. Loisy's *Essais* has since been published in Loisy, *La crise*.

18. Loisy, *Choses passées*, 246. Later he would amend this to, "Therefore I did not limit myself to criticizing Harnack, I implied with discretion, but directly, an essential reform of the received exegesis, of the official theology, of the ecclesiastical government in general." See Loisy, *Mémoires II*, 168.

19. Talar, "Reading of the Gospel," 306. See also Daly, "Theological and Philosophical," 106; and Talar, *Metaphor and Modernist*, 51, 102, and 107.

20. Talar, "Reading of the Gospel," 309. In other words, "Loisy mirrored

Consider the wording from *Lamentabili Sane Exitu* in number 52 and 53 of condemned propositions: "It was alien to the mind of Christ to constitute a Church as it were a society to continue on the earth for a long succession of ages; rather in the mind of Christ the kingdom of heaven with the end of the world was about to come imminently." And, "The organic constitution of the Church is not immutable; but Christian society undergoes the perpetual evolution to which human society is subjected."[21] *Lamentabili* had Loisy's words from *L'Évangile et l'Église* in mind here.[22] Claus Arnold confirms this when he writes, "The genesis of the decree *Lamentabili* comes directly from the preparatory work for the putting together of the Index of the principal works of Loisy that took place between 1901 and 1903, first at the Congregation of the Index, and then at the Holy Office."[23]

In *L'Évangile et l'Église* Loisy emphasized the eschatological aspect of the kingdom of God over the more moral aspect and the idea of the Kingdom as already present. This, however, represents a development of what he had earlier written in his unpublished

---

his own position in his criticism of Harnack. In regarding that reflection, the reader would be led to question the adequacy of the reigning Catholic theology" (309). And later, "In *L'Evangile et l'église* Loisy had engaged Harnack's position as a means of introducing his own" (314).

21. Latin text taken from Inquisition, "Quo sub 65," 476–77.

22. Arnold and Losito, ed., «*Lamentabili sane exitu*», 303, 303n347; and Arnold and Losito, ed., *La censure*, 159–60, 159n19, and 160n23, which document evidence that *Lamentabili* nos. 52–53 were taken from *L'Évangile et l'Église*. This evidence is taken from Louis Billot's vote at the Sacred Congregation of the Index on the status of Loisy's *L'Évangile et l'Église*. Billot translated lines from Loisy's work into Latin and those propositions eventually found their way into *Lamentabili*. Loisy surmised as much, that his works were what inspired *Lamentabili* (and in Pope St. Pius X's *Pascendi Dominici Gregis*), in Loisy, *Simples réflexions*, e.g., when he wrote, "My writings have provided the largest number of propositions censured by the Holy Office" (6). He saw the bulk of *Lamentabili* as directed against himself, especially what he wrote in *L'Évangile et l'Église*, but also in *Autour d'un petit livre*. His surmise remained unchanged in the second edition of *Simples réflexions* published that same year, Loisy, *Simples réflexions*, e.g., 6.

23. Arnold, "*Lamentabili sane exitu*. Le Magistère," 4. This essay is a revised version of Arnold, "Lamentabili sane exitu. Das Römische," 24–51.

Essais, wherein he combined both notions and cautioned against the kind of approach he himself would later take in *L'Évangile et l'Église*.[24] For example, in his earlier *Essais*, Loisy cautioned against just such a relegation of the kingdom to the realm of the eschatological that he appeared to make later in *L'Évangile et l'Église*. Thus, in *Essais* he wrote:

> On the other hand, one should not exaggerate the importance of the eschatological element to the point of denying the moral and present [*actuel*] element of the kingdom, of reducing it to a mere hope, or we will be eager to show it as a mere illusion, the conditions provided for its fulfillment having not been realized. Jesus speaks of the kingdom of heaven as being already present, and, in most cases, one cannot allege the influence of the apostolic tradition . . . One must keep these two elements together as belonging to the historical notion of the reign of God announced by Jesus.[25]

Harvey Hill observes:

> The more moral and less apocalyptic tone of Loisy's picture of Jesus appears most concretely in his different assessment of key biblical passages. In *L'Évangile et l'Église*, Loisy accused Harnack of basing his reconstruction on two passages . . . [Matt. 11:27 and Luke 17:21]. Both passages, Loisy claimed, stemmed from the early Church and could not, therefore, serve as convincing evidence for the views of the historical Jesus. In the "Essais," on the other hand, Loisy made claims strikingly similar to those he attacked in Harnack, and he based them on these same passages.[26]

What was the cause of Loisy's development in thought? Hill mentions that Loisy's *Essais* was indebted to the work of Heinrich

---

24. This was already noted by Hill, "Loisy's *L'Évangile*," 83, which first brought this to my attention. It should be noted that Loisy does concede some of this earlier view as possible in *L'Évangile et l'Église* (e.g., 36; ET 54), but it is primarily eclipsed by the eschatological notion.

25. Loisy, *La crise*, 171.

26. Hill, "Loisy's *L'Évangile*," 83.

Holtzmann. His shift cannot be reduced simply to rhetorical effect (considering the shared theological views of Holtzmann and Harnack coupled with Loisy's concern to critique Harnack in *L'Évangile et l'Église*). Rather, his preparation for teaching New Testament classes (which paved the way for his later Gospel commentaries) coincided with his revisions of *L'Évangile et l'Église*, and influenced his revisions.[27]

The Coming Kingdom

In contrast to his later work after his excommunication, where Loisy emphasized the broader Greco-Roman and especially mystery religions background to the New Testament, in *L'Évangile et l'Église*, Jesus, the Gospels, and the New Testament in general, are placed in the context of second temple Judaism.[28] Loisy did this even for the apostle Paul.[29] He also situated the language of "son of God" in this Jewish messianic context.[30] Occasionally, Loisy made an additional link between second temple Jewish thought and earlier non-Jewish influences, as with the concept of resurrection stemming from Persian influence.[31] Loisy saw Christian baptism

---

27. Hill, "Loisy's *L'Évangile*," 84. It is interesting to note that, although Holtzmann does not appear explicitly in *L'Évangile et l'Église*, Loisy did cite Holtzmann (6 times) in the sections of his unpublished *Essais* that eventually went into *L'Évangile et l'Église*. Moreover, in Loisy, Études évangeliques, published the same year as the first edition of *L'Évangile et l'Église*, Loisy cited Holtzmann, or one of Holtzmann's publications, 54 times. The only single author in Études évangeliques whom Loisy cited more than Holtzmann was Adolf Jülicher (with 73 citations).

28. For Loisy's comments situating Jesus in his Jewish context, see, e.g., Loisy, *L'Évangile et l'Église*, 105–7 (ET 120–21). For Loisy's later post-1908 use of parallels from the mystery religions, in which he was influenced by the work of the Belgian History of Religions scholar Franz Cumont, see, e.g., Praet and Lannoy, "Alfred Loisy's Comparative Method," 64–96; Lannoy, "Comparing Words," 111–25; Praet, "Symbolisme," 127–42; Lannoy, "St Paul," 222–39; and Lannoy, "La correspondance," 261–65.

29. E.g., Loisy, *L'Évangile et l'Église*, 25 (ET 45).

30. E.g., Loisy, *L'Évangile et l'Église*, 76 (ET 91).

31. E.g., Loisy, *L'Évangile et l'Église*, 122–26 (ET 135–38).

as rooted in Judaism.³² Loisy denied, however, a Jewish context for the Eucharist at the Last Supper.³³ In short, Loisy detected a second temple Jewish matrix for virtually the whole of the New Testament. Loisy's stance might be summarized in his statement on how much the Old Testament influenced the New Testament: "it colors most of its stories."³⁴

Loisy thus criticized Harnack for de-Judaizing early Christianity: "Thus it is quite arbitrary to declare that Christianity must be essentially whatever the Gospel has not borrowed from Judaism, as if whatever the Gospel has retained of the Jewish tradition was necessarily of secondary value."³⁵ This is consistent with Loisy's later criticism of Harnack for attempting to remove the so-called "husk" [*Schale*] of the tradition of Israel from the "kernel" [*Kern*] of the Gospel's portrayal of faith in God.³⁶ Writing further, Loisy underscored that, "Jesus has claimed not to destroy the Law, but to fulfill it. We must therefore expect to find, in Judaism and in Christianity, common elements, essential to the one and to the other, the difference between the two religions is in the 'fulfillment' that is specific to the Gospel, and which, joined to the common elements, must form the total essence of Christianity."³⁷

Throughout *L'Évangile et l'Église*, Loisy placed a strong emphasis on this Jewish context, which stands out in the context of the time, when so many French (think Renan) and German scholars

---

32. Loisy, *L'Évangile et l'Église*, 239 (ET 242).

33. Loisy, *L'Évangile et l'Église*, 234 (ET 238). The most robust and sophisticated recent study examining the Last Supper accounts within the context of second temple Judaism is Pitre, *Jesus and the Last Supper*.

34. Loisy, *L'Évangile et l'Église*, 24 (ET 43). When it came to the Church, however, Loisy was very clear that historical circumstances led to its development increasingly removed from Judaism (226; ET 231).

35. Loisy, *L'Évangile et l'Église*, XVI (ET 10).

36. Loisy, *L'Évangile et l'Église*, 45–46 (ET 63). German from Harnack, *Das Wesen*, 36.

37. Loisy, *L'Évangile et l'Église*, XVIII (ET 10–11). Further on, in the initial additional chapter on Gospel sources absent from his first edition, Loisy emphasized the second temple Jewish background, and in particular the book of Daniel, to the Gospel of John's chronology (12–13; ET 33–34).

were de-emphasizing the Jewish context of the New Testament, as Loisy also would later do after his excommunication.[38] In *L'Évangile et l'Église*, Loisy wrote, "The Gospel, appearing in Judaea, unable to appear anywhere else, also had to be conditioned by Judaism [*judaïquement*]. Its Jewish exterior is the human body of which the spirit of Jesus is the divine soul. But remove the body, and the soul will vanish in the air like the lightest breath."[39] And again, he explained, closer to the end of his volume, "Christian thought, in its beginning, was Jewish and could not but be Jewish . . ."[40] Indeed, Loisy went so far as to write, "The Gospel, as such, was nothing but a religious movement which was produced within Judaism, to realize perfectly its [Judaism's] principles and hopes."[41]

It is partly in this context of Jesus emerging from within his second temple Jewish milieu that Loisy emphasized the almost completely eschatological nature of the kingdom of God in *L'Évangile et l'Église*. The other context for this focus on the kingdom pertained to Loisy's views on doctrinal development, in this case the development of ecclesiology, as well as his concern for reform. Against what he took as a Protestant (in Harnack and Louis Auguste Sabatier) overemphasis on the individual, Loisy asserted the more communal notion of society and community, as when he wrote: "the Gospel of Jesus already had a rudiment of social organization, and . . . the kingdom was also to be a form of society. Jesus announced the kingdom, and it is the Church that came. She came by expanding the form of the Gospel, which was impossible to keep such as it was, as soon as the ministry of Jesus

---

38. On Renan in this context, see the comments in Masuzawa, *Invention of World Religions*, 171–78. Renan linked Christianity with Judaism, but in such a way that Judaism was lesser than Christianity and was superseded by Christianity. He wrote that Christianity came from Judaism, but that, "Christianity once produced, Judaism still continues, but as a desiccated trunk alongside the only fertile branch. From now on the life has left it." Renan, *Histoire du peuple* 5, 414–15. This is notwithstanding the fact that Renan called Christianity the "masterpiece" [*chef-d'oeuvre*] of Judaism (415).

39. Loisy, *L'Évangile et l'Église*, 106 (ET 121).

40. Loisy, *L'Évangile et l'Église*, 178 (ET 188).

41. Loisy, *L'Évangile et l'Église*, 225 (ET 230).

was closed by the passion."[42] Those comments form the proximate context for his infamous statement, "Jesus foretold the kingdom, and it was the Church that came."

Loisy's entire second chapter (the first in his 1902 edition) was devoted to the kingdom of heaven, or the kingdom of God. This is what Loisy identified as the "normal [*ordinaire*] theme" of Jesus' preaching.[43] Indeed, "All of his teachings are given in view of the kingdom."[44] In the Jewish context in which Loisy situated this, particularly in the Book of Daniel, Loisy saw this view of the kingdom as inherently eschatological, pointing to the end of the world.[45] Indeed, the promised kingdom, as a future as yet unfulfilled event, occupies much of Loisy's section here.[46] Later in his volume he stated emphatically, "the kingdom is essentially to come."[47] In light of Loisy's earlier comment that Jesus "assures his disciples that many of them will still be alive when the kingdom comes," it appears Loisy, like so many New Testament scholars, envisioned a Jesus conscious of an imminent end of the world.[48]

The Catholic Hierarchy and the Universal Possibility of Holiness

How does all of this relate to the Church? As Loisy's chapter on the Church indicated, he did in fact view the Church in some relation to the coming kingdom of God. The Church, as a continuation of

---

42. Loisy, *L'Évangile et l'Église*, 155 (ET 166).
43. Loisy, *L'Évangile et l'Église*, 35 (ET 53).
44. Loisy, *L'Évangile et l'Église*, 35 (ET 53).
45. Loisy, *L'Évangile et l'Église*, 35–36 (ET 53–54).
46. E.g., Loisy, *L'Évangile et l'Église*, 38–39, 41–42, and 44–45 (ET 56–57 and 59–62).
47. Loisy, *L'Évangile et l'Église*, 87 (ET 102). The full sentence reads, "As the kingdom is essentially to come, the role of the Messiah is essentially eschatological."
48. Loisy, *L'Évangile et l'Église*, 39 (ET 57). For a more recent challenge to this near consensus, see the published doctoral dissertation, Pitre, *Jesus, the Tribulation*.

the original society of Jesus' disciples, ever adapting to the new historical situations in which it found itself, was, for Loisy, "the anticipation of the kingdom of heaven."[49] In the context of discussing the Eucharist, Loisy admitted that, "the thought [*regard*] of Jesus was not directly embracing the idea of a new religion, of founding a Church, but rather realizing the kingdom of heaven."[50]

In contrast to Harnack, Loisy viewed the Church's hierarchical structure as a natural development from the original society of Jesus' disciples. In fact, Loisy presented a sort of history of development where the earliest community, in response to the historical pressures of the times, developed various levels of authority structures.[51] Loisy viewed such a hierarchical structure, albeit in small acorn-like form, already present in Jesus' life among the twelve.[52] The specifics of future or present hierarchical structures in the Church, Loisy maintained, were not present in Jesus' mind or preaching, nor could they have been. Such developments, which he argued were important and necessary, were developments required by the vicissitudes of history.[53]

This discussion brings us to Loisy's larger concern for reform. He brought up Church reform explicitly in *L'Évangile et l'Église*.[54] After recounting some of the political history in which the Church was caught up,[55] Loisy emphasized that the Church was primarily evangelistic and not political.[56] One wonders if his contemporary Church-state conflicts, and particularly those over

---

49. Loisy, *L'Évangile et l'Église*, 110 (ET 125).

50. Loisy, *L'Évangile et l'Église*, 226 (ET 231).

51. Loisy, *L'Évangile et l'Église*, 133-39, 141, 154-55, and 240-41 (ET 146-51, 153, 165, and 236-37).

52. Loisy, *L'Évangile et l'Église*, 133-36 (ET 146-48). Loisy did not explicitly link this structure with earlier second temple Jewish precedents. Some more recent scholars have done precisely this in some very interesting ways. See, e.g., Barber, "Jesus as Davidic Temple Builder," 935-53.

53. Loisy, *L'Évangile et l'Église*, 155 and 157 (ET 166-67).

54. E.g., Loisy, *L'Évangile et l'Église*, 152 (ET 162-63).

55. Loisy, *L'Évangile et l'Église*, 153 (ET 163-64).

56. Loisy, *L'Évangile et l'Église*, 161-64 (ET 172-74).

education, loomed in the background of Loisy's comments here.[57] In fact, once Loisy's own contemporary political background during the time of his writing and publishing *L'Évangile et l'Église* is considered, one wonders how much of his reform (political and ecclesiastical) is part of the overall background to his volume.[58] For my part, I think it plays a significant role.

A part of Loisy's reform agenda appears to have been deeply spiritual.[59] In what appears to be an anticipation of the Second Vatican Council's teaching on the universal call to holiness, Loisy wrote, "God is not further from the faithful than from the bishop or from the priest. Clergy and laity go to God together, pray together, are sanctified together."[60] These words may not sound very controversial to post-Vatican II Catholic readers. But I think it is easy to underestimate how radical and perhaps even dangerous these words could have appeared to some of Loisy's contemporaries. Something similar might be said about Loisy's comment, "The faithful do not exist to serve the hierarchy, but the hierarchy exists to serve the faithful."[61] This reforming agenda might change the way we read Loisy's earlier passages concerning the Gospel as preparation for the future kingdom.[62] It is even possible that some of what he wrote was intended as an examination of conscience of sorts directed at members of the Catholic hierarchy. Jesus' "Repent, for the kingdom of heaven is at hand,"

---

57. On Loisy's thoughts concerning education in France and the Church-state conflicts surrounding education, see, e.g., Hill, "Loisy's 'Mystical Faith,'" 73–94; Hill, "Politics," 170–72 and 176–89; and Hill, "French Politics," 521–36, esp. 529–32.

58. Hill, "Loisy's 'Mystical Faith,'" 73–94; Hill, "More than a Biblical Critic," 705–7; Hill, "Politics," 169–90; and Hill, "French Politics," 521–36.

59. Maude Petre depicted Loisy, even after his excommunication, as a deeply spiritual figure. See Petre, *Alfred Loisy*; Hill, "Maude Petre," 834–51; and Jacobs, "Last Modernist."

60. Loisy, *L'Évangile et l'Église*, 265 (ET 265).

61. Loisy, *L'Évangile et l'Église*, 164 (ET 173–74).

62. Loisy, *L'Évangile et l'Église*, 35, 42, and 44 (ET 53 and 60–61).

would take on a whole new meaning if this reforming agenda were the appropriate context in which to read it.[63]

Conclusion

In its time, *L'Évangile et l'Église* received criticisms from every corner; the most trenchant perhaps were leveled by Maurice Blondel.[64] I think, however, Hill is right when he concludes that, "*L'Évangile et l'Église* did not stand alone, but rather was one step in the program of theological reform that Loisy developed at much greater length in the 'Essais.'"[65] Obviously, as the quotation from *Lumen Gentium* with which I opened this chapter indicates, Loisy's volume would not be affirmed *in toto* by the Second Vatican Council. But I do think there are some ways in which he stands as part of a broader movement that paved the way to Vatican II, particularly in his comments on the universal potential for sanctity. More work remains to be done here, but I think that Loisy's work is one part of a much larger and diverse stream, a stream that includes the Paulists, the Salesians of Don Bosco, Opus Dei, and others, that were attempting to re-envision the role of the hierarchy, the laity, and the search for holiness in the world. They did not all take the same path, but there was something similar about what they were trying to achieve, despite their many differences. Loisy's hope for reform was much broader, I think, than simply biblical scholarship or scholastic theology. The ecclesiology of *L'Évangile et l'Église* formed a part of that reform effort.

---

63. Loisy, *L'Évangile et l'Église*, 38 (ET 56).

64. On Blondel's correspondence with Loisy, including concerns with *L'Évangile et l'Église*, see Izquierdo, "Correspondencia," 199–227; Ciappa, *Rivelazione e storia*; Izquierdo, *Blondel*, 123–68; Resch, "History and Dogma," 35–55; and Poulat, *Histoire, dogme, et critique*, 513–33 and 548–66.

65. Hill, "More than a Biblical Critic," 704.

Conclusion

THOSE LABELLED "MODERNIST" ARE of an incredibly wide variety. Modernism as a unified and well-orchestrated revolutionary movement within the Catholic Church at the dawn of the twentieth-century, does not seem to have existed, at least in any monolithic and unified way. At the same time, there clearly were individuals who fit the intellectual profile *Pascendi Dominic Gregis* painted. From the standpoint of intellectual history, those as diverse as Alfred Loisy, George Tyrrell, Baron Friedrich von Hügel, Maurice Blondel, Marie-Joseph Lagrange—clearly a diverse group, but whom some anti-modernists considered to be modernist—were concerned with the subjective "knower" (and not merely what was "known"), and were likewise interested in using modern critical methods in their investigation of theology and Scripture.

Modernism as a field of inquiry is as relevant as ever, not merely because of contemporary debates about the continued presence of modernism in the post-Vatican II Catholic Church,[1] but also because of the importance it has in understanding the history of twentieth century Catholic theology, especially leading up to the Second Vatican Council, universally recognized as

---

1. See, e.g., comments in Kirwan, *Avant-garde Theological Generation*; and Mettepenningen, *Nouvelle Théologie*.

a watershed event within the Catholic Church. Alfred Loisy has been at the forefront of this debate, even as he was at the forefront of the initial controversy,[2] in part because he has been the focus of much of my own work.[3] He is far from the only important figure within this history.

Much more work remains to be done within the study of Roman Catholic Modernism. Even as concerns Loisy, there remains no critical biography of Loisy. Archival work on the anti-modernist responses to figures like Loisy, have uncovered a wealth of resources helping shed light on the condemnations of Loisy and his works' being placed on the Index of Forbidden Books,[4] the Holy Office's decree *Lamentabili Sane Exitu* of 1907,[5] and the formation of Pope St. Pius X's 1907 *Pascendi Dominici Gregis*.[6] These and related studies continue to shed light on the broader context of what was going on behind the scenes and help complete our picture of the modernist crisis.

Studying this time period helps us better understand what has come before, but, more than this, it helps us understand the ways in which our theological intellectual forebears wrestled with challenges that, in some regard, remain perennial, namely the relationship between faith and reason, the integration of new scholarly findings and methods, and the faith which is both ancient and ever new.

2. See, e.g., Arnold and Losito, ed., *La censure*.
3. Especially Morrow, *Alfred Loisy*.
4. Arnold and Losito, ed., *La censure*.
5. Arnold and Losito, ed., «*Lamentabili sane exitu*».
6. Arnold and Vian, ed., *La Redazione*.

Bibliography

Åkerman, Susanna. *Queen Christina of Sweden and Her Circle: The Transformation of a Seventeenth-Century Philosophical Libertine*. Brill's Studies in Intellectual History 21. Leiden: Brill, 1991.
Aling, Charles F. "The Biblical City of Ramses." *Journal of the Evangelical Theological Society* 25 (1982) 129–37.
———. *Egypt and Bible History: From Earliest Times to 1000 B.C.* Grand Rapids: Baker, 1981.
———. "Some Remarks on the Historicity of the Joseph Story." *Near Eastern Archaeological Society Bulletin* 39–40 (1995) 31–37.
———. "The Sphinx Stele of Thutmose IV and the Date of the Exodus." *Journal of the Evangelical Theological Society* 22 (1979) 97–101.
Allen, Douglas. "Eliade's Phenomenological Approach to Religion and Myth." In *Mircea Eliade: Myth, Religion, and History*, edited by Nicolae Babuts, 85–112. New Brunswick: Transaction, 2014.
———. *Myth and Religion in Mircea Eliade*. Theorists of Myth 11. New York: Garland, 1998.
Arnold, Bill T., and David W. Weisberg. "Babel und Bibel und Bias: How Anti-Semitism Distorted Friedrich Delitzsch's Scholarship." *Bible Review* 18.1 (2002) 32–40 and 47.
———. "A Centennial Review of Friedrich Delitzsch's 'Babel und Bibel' Lectures." *Journal of Biblical Literature* 121 (2002) 441–57.
———. "A Centennial Review of *Die Große Täuschung*: Friedrich Delitzsch's Final Reflections on the Bable-Bibel Controversy." In *Der Babel-Bibel-Streit und die Wissenschaft des Judentums: Beiträge einer internationalen Konferenz vom 4. bis 6. November 2019 in Berlin*, edited by Eva Cancik-Kirschbaum and Thomas L. Gertzen, 45–61. Münster: Zaphon, 2021.

——. "Delitzsch in Context." In *God's Word for Our World Volume II: Theological and Cultural Studies in Honor of Simon De Vries*, edited by J. Harold Ellens, Deborah L. Ellens, Rolf P. Knierim, and Isaac Kalimi, 37–45. Journal for the Study of the Old Testament Supplements 389. London: T. & T. Clark, 2004.

Arnold, Claus. "*Lamentabili sane exitu* (1907). Le Magistère romain et l'exégèse d'Alfred Loisy." In «*Lamentabili sane exitu*» (1907). *Les documents préparatoires du Saint Office*, edited by Claus Arnold and Giacomo Losito. Rome: Libreria Editrice Vaticana, 2011.

——. "'*Lamentabili sane exitu*' (1907). Das Römische Lehramt und die Exegese Alfred Loisy." *Zeitschrift für Neuere Theologiegeschichte* 11 (2004) 24–51.

——. "Newman and '*Modernism*': A Matter of Definition?" *Newman Studies Journal* 20.2 (2023) 11–25.

——. "The Roman Magisterium and Anti-Modernism." In *Religious Modernism in the Low Countries*, edited by Leo Kenis and Ernestine van der Wall, 159–69. Bibliotheca Ephemeridum theologicarum Lovaniensium 255. Leuven: Peeters, 2013.

Arnold, Claus, and Giacomo Losito, edited by *La censure d'Alfred Loisy (1903): Les documents des Congrégations de l'Index et du Saint Office*. Rome: Libreria Editrice Vaticana, 2009.

——, ed. «*Lamentabili sane exitu*» (1907). *Les documents préparatoires du Saint Office*. Rome: Libreria Editrice Vaticana, 2011.

Arnold, Claus, Francesco Tacchi, and Giovanni Vian. *The Controversy over Integralism in Germany, Italy and France during the Pontificate of Pius X (1903–1914)*. Bibliothèque de la Revue d'histoire ecclésiastique 116. Turnhout: Brepols, 2024.

Arnold, Claus, and Gioanni Vian, eds. *La Redazione dell'Enciclica Pascendi: Studi e documenti sull'antimodernismo di Papa Pio X*. Päpste und Papsttum 48. Stuttgart: Hierse-mann, 2020.

Art, Jan. "La crise moderniste et l'opinion libérale: le cas de Gand." In *Science, Religion and Politics during the Modernist Crisis/Science, Religion et Politique à l'époque de la Crise Moderniste*, edited by Danny Praet and Corinne Bonnet, 313–37. Institut Historique Belge de Rome Études 5. Brussels and Rome: Istituto Storico Belga di Roma, 2018.

Asad, Talal. *Formations of the Secular: Christianity, Islam, Modernity*. Cultural Memory in the Present. Stanford: Stanford University Press, 2003.

——. *Genealogies of Religion: Discipline and Reasons of Power in Christianity and Islam*. Baltimore: Johns Hopkins University Press, 1993.

Barber, Michael Patrick. "Jesus as Davidic Temple Builder and Peter's Priestly Role in Matthew 16:16–19." *Journal of Biblical Literature* 132 (2013) 935–53.

Barmann, Lawrence. "The Pope and the English Modernists." *U.S. Catholic Historian* 25.1 (2007) 31–54.

BIBLIOGRAPHY

Barmann, Lawrence F., and C. J. T. Talar, eds. *Sanctity and Secularity during the Modernist Period: Six Perspectives on Hagiography around 1900/ Six perspectives sur l'hagiographie aux alentours de 1900*. Subsidia hagiographica 79. Brussels: Société des Bollandistes, 1999.

Barmann, Lawrence, and Harvey Hill, eds. *Personal Faith and Institutional Commitments: Roman Catholic Modernist and Anti-Modernist Autobiography*. Scranton, PA: University of Scranton Press, 2002.

Bea, Augustin. *De Pentateucho*. Institutiones Biblicae scholis accommodatae 2. Rome: Pontifical Biblical Institute Press, 1928.

Beidelman, T. O. *W. Robertson Smith and the Sociological Study of Religion*. Chicago: University of Chicago Press, 1974.

Bergsma, John S., and Jeffrey L. Morrow. *Murmuring Against Moses: The Contentious History and Contested Future of Pentateuchal Studies*. Steubenville, OH: Emmaus Academic, 2023.

Bernardi, Peter J., SJ. "Maurice Blondel: Precursor of the Second Vatican Council." *Josephinum Journal of Theology* 22 (2015) 59–77.

———. *Maurice Blondel, Social Catholicism, & Action Française: The Clash over the Church's Role in Society during the Modernist Era*. Washington, DC: Catholic University of America Press, 2008.

Blanchette, Oliva. *Maurice Blondel: A Philosophical Life*. Grand Rapids: Eerdmans, 2010.

Block, Daniel I. "Editors' Preface and Acknowledgements." In *Write That They May Read: Studies in Literacy and Textualization in the Ancient Near East and in the Hebrew Scriptures: Essays in Honour of Professor Alan R. Millard*, edited by Daniel I. Block, David C. Deuel, C. John Collins, and Paul J. N. Lawrence, xv–xvii. Eugene, OR: Pickwick Publications, 2020.

———. Introduction to *Write That They May Read: Studies in Literacy and Textualization in the Ancient Near East and in the Hebrew Scriptures: Essays in Honour of Professor Alan R. Millard*, edited by Daniel I. Block et al., xxix–xxxiv. Eugene, OR: Pickwick Publications, 2020.

Blondel, Maurice. *The Letter on Apologetics and History and Dogma*. Edited and translated by Alexander Dru and Illtyd Trethowan. Grand Rapids: Eerdmans, 1994.

Bonnet, Corinne. "L'«affaire Cumont» entre science, politique et religion." In *Science, Religion and Politics during the Modernist Crisis/Science, Religion et Politique à l'époque de la Crise Moderniste*, ed. Danny Praet and Corinne Bonnet, 403–17. Institut Historique Belge de Rome Études 5. Brussels and Rome: Istituto Storico Belga di Roma, 2018.

Botti, Alfonso and Rocco Cerrato, edited by *Il modernismo tra cristianità e secolarizzazione*. Urbino: Quattro Venti, 2000.

Boyd, J. O. "Ezekiel and the Modern Dating of the Pentateuch." *Princeton Theological Review* 6 (1908) 29–51.

Burke, Ronald. "Was Loisy Newman's Modern Disciple?" In *Newman and the Modernists*, edited by Mary Jo Weaver, 139–57. Lanham, MD: University Press of America, 1985.

BIBLIOGRAPHY

Calvert, Kenneth R. "Edwin M. Yamauchi." In *The Light of Discovery: Studies in Honor of Edwin M. Yamauchi*, edited by John D. Wineland, 1–23. Eugene, OR: Pickwick Publicatoins, 2007.

Carmignac, Jean. *Le mirage de l'Eschatologie*. Paris: Letouzey et Ané,1979.

Cassuto, Umberto. *La questione della Genesi*. Florence: Le Monnier, 1934.

Cavanaugh, William T. "'A Fire Strong Enough to Consume the House:' The Wars of Religion and the Rise of the State." *Modern Theology* 11 (1995) 397–420.

———. "Killing for the Telephone Company: Why the Nation-State is Not the Keeper of the Common Good." *Modern Theology* 20 (2004) 243–74.

———. *The Myth of Religious Violence: Secular Ideology and the Roots of Modern Conflict*. Oxford: Oxford University Press, 2009.

Chanel, Christian. "Les sciences de la religion au secour de l'Église: le modèle suédois et ses limites (1890–1914)." In *Science, Religion and Politics during the Modernist Crisis/Science, Religion et Politique à l'époque de la Crise Moderniste*, edited by Danny Praet and Corinne Bonnet, 117–55. Institut Historique Belge de Rome Études 5. Brussels and Rome: Istituto Storico Belga di Roma, 2018.

Chen, Y. S. *The Primeval Flood Catastrophe: Origins and Early Development in Mesopotamian Traditions*. Oxford: Oxford University Press, 2013.

Ciappa, Rosanna. *Rivelazione e storia. Il problema ermeneutico nel carteggio tra Alfred Loisy e Maurice Blondel (febbraio-marzo 1903)*. Naples: Università di Napoli, 2001.

Colin, Pierre. *L'audace et le soupçon. La crise moderniste dans le catholicisme français (1893–1914)*. Paris: Desclée de Brouwer, 1997.

———. "Le Kantisme dans la crise moderniste." In *Le modernisme*, edited by Dominique Dubarle, 9–81. Paris: Beauchesne, 1980.

———. *Morale et religion au temps de la crise moderniste. Études d'histoire de la philosophie française (XIXe et XXe siècles)*. Ed. Hubert Faes. Louvain-la-Neuve: Presses Universitaires de Louvain, 2017.

Collins, John J. *The Invention of Judaism: Torah and Jewish Identity from Deuteronomy to Paul*. Oakland: University of California Press, 2017.

Congar, Yves. *Journal of a Theologian*. Translated by Denis Minns. Adelaide: ATF, 2005.

Courtois, Luc. "Le chanoine Philémon Colinet (1853–1917) et la première Semaine d'ethnologie religieuse de Louvain (1911–1912): première approche d'une réaction antimoderniste." In *Science, Religion and Politics during the Modernist Crisis/Science, Religion et Politique à l'époque de la Crise Moderniste*, edited by Danny Praet and Corinne Bonnet, 221–49. Institut Historique Belge de Rome Études 5. Brussels and Rome: Istituto Storico Belga di Roma, 2018.

Daly, Gabriel. "Theological and Philosophical Modernism." In *Catholicism Contending with Modernity: Roman Catholic Modernism and Anti-Modernism in Historical Context*, edited by Darrell Jodock, 88–112. Cambridge: Cambridge University Press, 2000.

———. *Transcendence and Immanence: A Study in Catholic Modernism and Integralism*. Oxford: Oxford University Press, 1980.

D'Costa, Gavin. *Theology in the Public Square: Church, Academy, and Nation*. Oxford: Wiley-Blackwell, 2005.

De Maeyer, Jan, and Leo Kenis. "La création d'une intelligentsia catholique en Belgique dans la perspective de la «crise moderniste». L'optique du cardinal Désiré Mercier." In *Science, Religion and Politics during the Modernist Crisis/Science, Religion et Politique à l'époque de la Crise Moderniste*, edited by Danny Praet and Corinne Bonnet, 179–92. Institut Historique Belge de Rome études 5. Brussels and Rome: Istituto Storico Belga di Roma, 2018.

De Pril, Ward. "Modernism and the Problematic Relation between History and Theology. The Search for a Compromise by Louvain Historians and Theologians (1870–1910)." *Church History and Religious Culture* 91 (2011) 377–96.

Dietrich, Wendell S. "Loisy and the Liberal Protestants." *Studies in Religion/Sciences religieuses* 14 (1985) 303–11.

Ellwood, Robert S. "Eliade: Essentialist or Postmodern? The Sacred and an Unseen Order." In *Mircea Eliade: Myth, Religion, and History*, edited by Nicolae Babuts, 1–22. New York: Routledge, 2014.

———. *The Politics of Myth: A Study of C. G. Jung, Mircea Eliade, and Joseph Campbell*. Albany: State University of New York, 1999.

Feil, Ernst. "From the Classical *Religio* to the Modern *Religion*: Elements of a Transformation between 1550 and 1650." In *Religion in History: The Word, the Idea, the Reality*, edited by Michel Despland and Gérard Vallée, 31–43. Waterloo: Wilfrid Laurier University Press, 1992.

———. *Religio: Die Geschichte eines neuzeitlichen Grundbegriffs vom Frühchristentum bis zur Reformation*. Göttingen: Vandenhoeck & Ruprecht, 1986.

———. *Religio Zweiter Band: Die Geschichte eines neuzeitlichen Grundbegriffs zwischen Reformation und Rationalismus (ca. 1540–1620)*. Göttingen: Vandenhoeck & Ruprecht, 1997.

———. *Religio: Dritter Band: Die Geschichte eines neuzeitlichen Grundbegriffs im 17. und frühen 18. Jahrhundert*. Göttingen: Vandenhoeck & Ruprecht, 2001.

———. *Religio: Vierter Band: Die Geschichte eines neuzeitlichen Grundbegriffs im 18. und 19. Jahrhundert*. Göttingen: Vandenhoeck & Ruprecht, 2007.

Feldman, Louis H. "Homer and the Near East: The Rise of the Greek Genius." *Biblical Archaeologist* 59 (1996) 13–21.

Feller, Yaniv. "The Specter of Marcion: Decanonizing the Old Testament in Twenty-First-Century Germany." *Journal of Religion* 103 (2023) 409–30.

Fogarty, Gerald P. *American Catholic Biblical Scholarship: A History from the Early Republic to Vatican II*. San Francisco: Harper & Row, 1989.

Geyer, Carl-Friedrich. *Wahrheit und Absolutheit des Christentums—Geschichte und Utopie: „L'Évangile et l'Église" von Alfred F. Loisy in Text und Kontext*. Göttingen: Vandenhoeck & Ruprecht, 2010.

Gigot, Francis E. *General Introduction to the Study of the Holy Scriptures*. 3rd rev. ed. New York: Benziger Brothers, 1903.

———. *The Message of Moses and Modern Higher Criticism*. New York: Benziger, 1915.

Gillespie, Michael Allen. *The Theological Origins of Modernity*. Chicago: University of Chicago Press, 2008.

Ginzburg, Carlo. "Mircea Eliade's Ambivalent Legacy." In *Hermeneutics, Politics, and the History of Religions: The Contested Legacies of Joachim Wach and Mircea Eliade*, edited by Christian K. Wedemeyer and Wendy Doniger, 307–24. Oxford: Oxford University Press, 2010.

Gordon, Cyrus H. *A Scholar's Odyssey*. Biblical Scholarship in North America 20. Atlanta: Society of Biblical Literature, 2000.

Gregory, Brad S. *The Unintended Reformation: How a Religious Revolution Secularized Society*. Cambridge: Harvard University Press, 2012.

Gross, Michael B. *The War Against Catholicism: Liberalism and the Anti-Catholic Imagination in Nineteenth-Century Germany*. Ann Arbor: University of Michigan Press, 2004.

Hahn, Scott W., and Jeffrey L. Morrow. *Modern Biblical Criticism as a Tool of Statecraft (1700–1900)*. Steubenville, OH: Emmaus Academic, 2020.

Hallo, William W. "The Limits of Skepticism." *Journal of the American Oriental Society* 110 (1990) 187–99.

———. "New Viewpoints on Cuneiform Literature." *Israel Exploration Journal* 12 (1962) 13–26.

Harnack, Adolf. *Das Wesen des Christentums*. 5th ed. Leipzig: Hinrichs, 1902.

Harrison, Peter. *'Religion' and the Religions in the English Enlightenment*. Cambridge: Cambridge University Press, 1990.

Hauerwas, Stanley. *The State of the University: Academic Knowledges and the Knowledge of God*. Oxford: Wiley-Blackwell, 2007.

———. *With the Grain of the Universe: The Church's Witness and Natural Theology*. Grand Rapids: Baker Academic, 2001.

Hill, Harvey. "French Politics and Alfred Loisy's Modernism." *Church History* 67 (1998) 521–36.

———. "Loisy's *L'Évangile et l'Église* in Light of the 'Essais.'" *Theological Studies* 67 (2006) 73–98.

———. "Loisy's 'Mystical Faith': Loisy, Leo XIII, and Sabatier on Moral Education and the Church." *Theological Studies* 65 (2004) 73–94.

———. "Maude Petre on Loisy's Religious Significance: Spirituality and Critical History." *Theological Studies* 69 (2008) 834–51.

———. "More than a Biblical Critic: Alfred Loisy's Modernism in Light of His Autobiographies." *Anglican Theological Review* 85 (2003) 689–707.

———. "The Politics of Loisy's Modernist Theology." In *Catholicism Contending with Modernity: Roman Catholic Modernism and Anti-Modernism in Historical Context*, edited by Darrell Jodock, 169–90. Cambridge: Cambridge University Press, 2000.

BIBLIOGRAPHY

Hoffmeier, James K. *Ancient Israel in Sinai: The Evidence for the Authenticity of the Wilderness Tradition*. Oxford: Oxford University Press, 2005.

———. "Egyptian Religious Influences on the Early Hebrews." In *"Did I Not Bring Israel Out of Egypt?": Biblical, Archaeological, and Egyptological Perspectives on the Exodus Narratives*, edited by James K. Hoffmeier et al., 1–36. Winona Lake, IN : Eisenbrauns, 2016.

———. "Egyptologists and the Israelite Exodus from Egypt." In *Israel's Exodus in Transdisciplinary Perspective: Text, Archaeology, Culture, and Geoscience*, edited by Thomas E. Levy et al., 197–208. New York: Springer, 2015.

———. "The Evangelical Contribution to Understanding the (Early) History of Ancient Israel in Recent Scholarship." *Bulletin for Biblical Research* 7.1 (1997) 77–89.

———. "The Exodus and Wilderness Narratives." In *Ancient Israel's History: An Introduction to Issues and Sources*, edited by Bill T. Arnold and Richard S. Hess, 46–90. Grand Rapids: Baker Academic, 2014.

———. *Israel in Egypt: The Evidence for the Authenticity of the Exodus Tradition*. Oxford: Oxford University Press, 1997.

———. "The Structure of Joshua 1–11 and the Annals of Thutmose III." In *Faith, Tradition, History: Old Testament Historiography in Its Near Eastern Context*, edited by A. R. Millard et al., 165–79. Winona Lake, IN: Eisenbrauns, 1994.

———. "Understanding Hebrew and Egyptian Military Texts: A Contextual Approach." In *the Context of Scripture Volume III: Archival Documents from the Biblical World*, edited by William W. Hallo and K. Lawson Younger, Jr., xxi–xxvii. Leiden: Brill, 2002.

Hoffmeier, James K., and Gary A. Rendsburg. "Pithom and Rameses (Exodus 1:11): Historical, Archaeological, and Linguistic Issues (Part I)." *Journal of Ancient Egyptian Interconnections* 33 (2022) 1–19.

Horkheimer, Max, and Theodor W. Adorno. *Dialectic of Enlightenment*. Translated by John Cumming. New York: Continuum, 2002 (1944).

———. *Dialectic of Enlightenment: Philosophical Fragments*. Edited by Gunzelin Schmid Noerr. Translated by Edmund Jephcott. Stanford: Stanford University Press, 2002 (1944).

Idel, Moshe. "The Camouflaged Sacred in Mircea Eliade's Self-Perception, Literature, and Scholarship." In *Hermeneutics, Politics, and the History of Religions: The Contested Legacies of Joachim Wach and Mircea Eliade*, edited by Christian K. Wedemeyer and Wendy Doniger, 159–96. Oxford: Oxford University Press, 2010.

Israel, Jonathan I. *Enlightenment Contested: Philosophy, Modernity, and the Emancipation of Man 1670–1752*. Oxford: Oxford University Press, 2006.

———. *Radical Enlightenment: Philosophy and the Making of Modernity 1650–1750*. Oxford: Oxford University Press, 2001.

Izquierdo, César. *Blondel y la crisis modernista*. Pamplona: Ediciones Universidad de Navarra, 1990.

———. "Correspondencia entre M. Blondel y A. Loisy a propósito de *L'Évangile et l'Église*." *Anuario de Historia de la Iglesia* 13 (2004) 199–227.
Jacobs, Joseph Harry. "The Last Modernist? The Spiritual Vision of Maude Dominica Petre." PhD diss., University of Dayton, 2003.
Jodock, Darrell, ed. *Catholicism Contending with Modernity: Roman Catholic Modernism and Anti-Modernism in Historical Context*. Cambridge: Cambridge University Press, 2000.
Johnson, Luke Timothy. "The Crisis in Biblical Scholarship." *Commonweal* 120.21 (1993) 18–21.
———. "So What's Catholic About It? The State of Catholic Biblical Scholarship." *Commonweal* 125.1 (1998) 12–16.
———. "What's Catholic About Catholic Biblical Scholarship?" In *The Future of Catholic Biblical Scholarship: A Constructive Conversation*, by Luke Timothy Johnson and William S. Kurz, SJ, 3–34. Grand Rapids: Eerdmans, 2002.
Jones, Andrew Willard. *Before Church and State: A Study of the Social Order in the Sacramental Kingdom of St. Louis IX*. Steubenville, OH: Emmaus Academic, 2017.
Jung, Dietrich. "Sociology, Protestant Theology, and the Concept of Modern Religion: William Robertson Smith and the 'Scientification' of Religion." *Journal of Religion in Europe* 8.3–4 (2015) 335–64.
Kaufmann, Yehezkel. *The Religion of Israel: From Its Beginnings to the Babylonian Exile*. Chicago: University of Chicago Press, 1960.
Kenis, Leo, and Ernestine van der Wal, eds. *Religious Modernism in the Low Countries*. Leuven: Peeters, 2013.
Kerr, Fergus. *Twentieth-Century Catholic Theologians*. Oxford: Blackwell, 2007.
Kirwan, Jon. *An Avant-garde Theological Generation: The Nouvelle Théologie and the French Crisis of Modernity*. Oxford: Oxford University Press, 2018.
Kitchen, Kenneth A. *Ancient Orient and Old Testament*. London: InterVarsity, 1966.
———. "The Aramaic of Daniel." In *Notes on Some Problems in the Book of Daniel*, edited by D. J. Wiseman, 31–79. London: Tyndale, 1965.
———. "The Controlling Role of External Evidence in Assessing the Historical Status of the Israelite United Monarchy." In *Windows into Old Testament History: Evidence, Argument, and the Crisis of "Biblical Israel"*, edited by V. Philips Long et al., 111–30. Grand Rapids: Eerdmans, 2002.
———. "External Textual Sources—Early Arabia." In *The Book of Kings: Sources, Composition, Historiography and Reception*, edited by Baruch Halpern and André Lemaire, 381–83. Vetus Testamentum Supplements 129. Leiden: Brill, 2010.
———. "External Textual Sources—Egypt." In *The Book of Kings: Sources, Composition, Historiography and Reception*, edited by Baruch Halpern and André Lemaire, 369–80. Vetus Testamentum Supplements 129. Leiden: Brill, 2010.

———. "External Textual Sources—Neo-Hittite States." In *The Book of Kings: Sources, Composition, Historiography and Reception*, edited by Baruch Halpern and André Lemaire, 365-68. Vetus Testamentum Supplements 129. Leiden: Brill, 2010.

———. "Genesis 12-50 in the Near Eastern World." In *He Swore an Oath: Biblical Themes from Genesis 12-50*, edited by Richard S. Hess et al., 67-92. London: Tyndale House, 1994.

———. "The Hieroglyphic Inscriptions of the Neo-Hittite States (c. 1200-700 BC): A Fresh Source of Background to the Hebrew Bible." In *The Old Testament in Its World*, edited by Robert Gordon and Johannes de Moor, 117-34. Old Testament Studies 52. Leiden: Brill, 2005.

———. *In Sunshine & Shadow*. Liverpool: Abercromby, 2016.

———. *On the Reliability of the Old Testament*. Grand Rapids: Eerdmans, 2003.

———. "The Patriarchal Age: Myth or History?" *Biblical Archaeology Review* 21.2 (1995) 48-57.

———. "The Philistines." In *Peoples of Old Testament Times*, edited by D. J. Wiseman, 53-78. Oxford: Clarendon, 1973.

———. "A Possible Mention of David in the Late Tenth Century BCE, and Deity *Dod as Dead as the Dodo?" *Journal for the Study of the Old Testament* 76 (1997) 29-44.

———. "Some Egyptian Background to the Old Testament." *Tyndale Bulletin* 5-6 (1960) 4-18.

Lagrange, M.-J. *M. Loisy et le modernisme: A propos des «Mémoires»*. Paris: Cerf, 1932.

Lahutsky, Nadia. "Paris and Jerusalem: Alfred Loisy and Père Lagrange on the Gospel of Mark." *Catholic Biblical Quarterly* 52 (1990) 444-66.

Lambert, W. G., and A. R. Millard. *Atrahasis: The Babylonian Story of the Flood*. Oxford: Clarendon, 1969.

Lannoy, Annelies. *Alfred Loisy and the Making of History of Religions: A Study of the Development of Religion in the Early 20th Century*. Berlin: de Gruyter, 2020.

———. "Comparing Words, Myths and Rituals: Alfred Loisy, Franz Cumont and the Case of 'Gaionas le δειπνοκρίτης.'" *Mythos* 7 (2013) 111-26.

———. "Le Congrès d'histoire du christianisme: Franz Cumont et Alfred Loisy face au visages divers de l'histoire des religions indépendante." In *Science, Religion and Politics during the Modernist Crisis/Science, Religion et Politique à l'époque de la Crise Moderniste*, edited by Danny Praet and Corinne Bonnet, 419-69. Institut Historique Belge de Rome Études 5. Brussels and Rome: Istituto Storico Belga di Roma, 2018.

———. "La correspondance bilatérale entre Alfred Loisy et Franz Cumont: brève présentation et projet d'édition." *Anabases* 13 (2011) 261-65.

———. "St Paul in the Early 20th Century History of Religions: 'The Mystic of Tarsus' and the Pagan Mystery Cults after the Correspondence of Franz Cumont and Alfred Loisy." *Zeitschrift* für Religions- und *Geistesgeschichte* 64 (2012) 222-39.

Laplanche, François. *La Bible en France: entre mythe et critique, 16e-19e siècle.* Paris: Michel, 1994.

Legaspi, Michael C. "Beginnings of Historical Criticism." In *Oxford History of Modern German Theology Volume 1: 1781-1848*, edited by Grant Kaplan and Kevin M. Vander Schel, 121-42. Oxford: Oxford University Press, 2023.

———. *The Death of Scripture and the Rise of Biblical Studies.* Oxford: Oxford University Press, 2010.

———. "From Thomasius to Semler: History, Civil Philosophy, and Theology in the German Enlightenment." In *Theology, History, and the Modern German University*, edited by Kevin M. Vander Schel and Michael P. DeJonge, 11-26. Tübingen: Mohr Siebeck, 2021.

Lehner, Ulrich L. *The Catholic Enlightenment: The Forgotten History of a Global Movement.* Oxford: Oxford University Press, 2016.

———. *Enlightenment Monks: The German Benedictines 1740-1803.* Oxford: Oxford University Press, 2011.

———. *On the Road to Vatican II: German Catholic Enlightenment and Reform of the Church.* Minneapolis: Fortress, 2016.

Lenormant, François. *Les origines de l'histoire d'après la Bible et les traditions des peoples orientaux I.* Paris: Maisonneuve, 1880.

Levenson, Jon D. *The Hebrew Bible, the Old Testament, and Historical Criticism: Jews and Christians in Biblical Studies.* Louisville: Westminster/John Knox, 1993.

Loisy, Alfred. *Autour d'un petit livre.* Paris: Picard, 1903.

———. "Avant-propos." *L'enseignement biblique* 1 (1892) v-xvi.

———. *Choses passées.* Paris: Émile Nourry, 1913.

———. *La crise de la foi dans le temps présent (Essais d'histoire et de philosophie religieuses).* Ed. François Laplanche. Turnhout: Brepols, 2010.

———. "La crise de la foi dans le temps présent. Essais d'histoire et de philosophie religieuses." In F. Laplanche (ed.), *Alfred Loisy, La crise de la foi dans le temps présent (Essais d'histoire det de philosophie religieuses)*, edited by François Laplanche, 35-491. Turnhout: Brepols, 2010.

———. "De la critique biblique." *L'enseignement biblique* 6 (1892) 1-16.

———. *L'Évangile et l'Église.* Paris: Picard, 1902.

———. *L'Évangile et l'Église.* 2nd ed. Bellevue: L'auteur, 1903.

———. "Les Évangiles." *L'enseignement biblique* 8 (1893) 17-64.

———. *Évangiles synoptiques I.* Amiens: Rousseau-Leroy, 1893.

———. "Les Évangiles synoptiques I." *L'enseignement biblique* 11 (1893) 1-76.

———. "Les Évangiles synoptiques II." *L'enseignement biblique* 12 (1893) 77-156.

———. "Les Évangiles synoptiques III-IV." *L'enseignement biblique* 13 (1894) 157-348.

———. *Études bibliques.* 2nd ed. Paris: Picard, 1901.

———. *Études évangeliques.* Paris: Picard, 1902.

BIBLIOGRAPHY

———. *The Gospel and the Church.* Trans. Christopher Home. New York: Scribner, 1912.

———. *Histoire du Canon de l'Ancien Testament.* Paris: Letouzey et Ané, 1890.

———. *Histoire du Canon du Nouveau Testament.* Paris: Maisonneuve, 1891.

———. *Histoire critique du texte et des versions de la Bible. Tome I: Histoire du texte hébreu de l'Ancien Testament. Livre I: Histoire critique du texte de l'Ancien Testament.* Amiens: Rousseau-Leroy, 1892.

———. *Histoire critique du texte et des versions de la Bible. Tome I: Histoire du texte hébreu de l'Ancien Testament. Livre II: Histoire critique des versions de l'Ancien Testament.* Amiens: Rousseau-Leroy, 1893.

———. "Histoire critique des versions de l'Ancien Testament I." *L'enseignement biblique* 7 (1893) 17–80.

———. "Histoire critique des versions de l'Ancien Testament II." *L'enseignement biblique* 7 (1893) 81–128.

———. "Histoire critique des versions de l'Ancien Testament III." *L'enseignement biblique* 9 (1893) 129–92.

———. "Histoire critique des versions de l'Ancien Testament IV." *L'enseignement biblique* 10 (1893) 193–245.

———. "Histoire critique du texte de l'Ancient Testament I." *L'enseignement biblique* 1 (1892) 1–76.

———. "Histoire critique du texte de l'Ancient Testament II." *L'enseignement biblique* 1 (1892) 77–156.

———. "Histoire critique du texte de l'Ancient Testament III." *L'enseignement biblique* 1 (1892) 157–236.

———. "Histoire critique du texte de l'Ancient Testament IV." *L'enseignement biblique* 1 (1892) 237–313.

———. "Le Livre de Job I." *L'enseignement biblique* 5 (1892) 1–87.

———. "Le Livre de Job II." *L'enseignement biblique* 6 (1892) 89–175.

———. *Le Livre de Job: Traduit de l'hébreu avec une introduction.* Amiens: Rousseau-Leroy, 1892.

———. *Mémoires pour servir a l'histoire religieuses de notre temps. Tome I. 1857–1900.* Paris: Nourry, 1930.

———. *Mémoires pour servir a l'histoire religieuse de notre temps Tome II: 1900–1908.* Paris: Nourry, 1931.

———. *Les mythes babyloniens et les premiers chapitres de la Genèse.* Paris: Alphonse Picard, 1901.

———. *Les mythes chaldéens de la création et du Déluge.* Amiens: Rousseau-Leroy, 1892.

———. "Les onze premiers chapitres de la Genèse." *L'enseignement biblique* 7 (1893) 1–16.

———. *Les Proverbes de Salomon.* Amiens: Rousseau-Leroy, 1890.

———. "Les Proverbes de Salomon I." *Revue des Religions* 2.5 (1890) 28–44.

———. "Les Proverbes de Salomon II." *Revue des Religions* 2.5 (1890) 97–115.

———. "Les Proverbes de Salomon III." *Revue des Religions* 2.5 (1890) 217–40.

BIBLIOGRAPHY

———. "La question biblique et l'inspiration des Écritures." *L'enseignement biblique* 12 (1892) 1–16.

———. "La question du canon des Écritures au Concile de Trente." *L'enseignement biblique* 10 (1893) 247–55.

———. *Simples réflexions sur le Décret du Saint-Office Lamentabili sane exitu et sur l'Encyclique Pascendi dominici gregis*. Ceffonds: L'auteur, 1908.

———. *Simples réflexions sur le Décret du Saint-Office Lamentabili sane exitu et sur l'Encyclique Pascendi dominici gregis*. 2nd ed. Ceffonds: L'auteur, 1908.

Losito, Giacomo. "État, Église et Université en France: la difficile adaptation des directives de l'encyclique *Pascendi* dans les études du clergé." In *Science, Religion and Politics during the Modernist Crisis/Science, Religion et Politique à l'époque de la Crise Moderniste*, edited by Danny Praet and Corinne Bonnet, 3–48. Institut Historique Belge de Rome Études 5. Brussels and Rome: Istituto Storico Belga di Roma, 2018.

Lubetski, Meir, and Claire Gottlieb. "'Forever Gordon': Portrait of a Master Scholar with a Global Perspective." *Biblical Archaeologist* 59 (1996) 2–12.

Machinist, Peter. "The Road Not Taken: Wellhausen and Assyriology." In *Homeland and Exile: Biblical and Ancient Near Eastern Studies in Honour of Bustenay Oded*, edited by Gershon Galil et al., 469–531. Vetus Testamentum Supplements 130. Leiden: Brill, 2009.

MacIntyre, Alasdair. *After Virtue: A Study of Moral Theory*. 3rd ed. Notre Dame, IN: University of Notre Dame Press, 2007 (1981).

———. *Three Rival Versions of Moral Enquiry: Encyclopaedia, Genealogy, and Tradition*. Notre Dame, IN: University of Notre Dame Press, 1990.

———. *Whose Justice? Which Rationality?* Notre Dame, IN: University of Notre Dame Press, 1988.

Maher, Anthony M. *The Forgotten Jesuit of Catholic Modernism: George Tyrrell's Prophetic Theology*. Minneapolis: Fortress, 2017.

Maier, Bernhard. *William Robertson Smith: His Life, His Work, and His Times*. Tübingen: Mohr Siebeck, 2009.

Maier, Paul L. Foreword to *The Light of Discovery: Studies in Honor of Edwin M. Yamauchi*, edited by John D. Wineland, xi–xiv. Eugene, OR: Pickwick Publications, 2007.

Mansini, Guy. "Experience and Discourse, Revelation and Dogma in Catholic Modernism." *Nova et Vetera* 17 (2019) 1119–43.

Marblestone, Howard. "A 'Mediterranean Synthesis': Professor Cyrus H. Gordon's Contributions to the Classics." *Biblical Archaeologist* 59 (1996) 22–30.

Marshner, William H., ed. *Defending the Faith: An Anti-Modernist Anthology*. Washington, DC: The Catholic University of America Press, 2017.

Maryanski, Alexandra. "The Birth of the Gods: Robertson Smith and Durkheim's Turn to Religion as the Basis of Social Integration." *Sociological Theory* 32 (2014) 352–76.

Masuzawa, Tomoko. *In Search of Dreamtime: The Quest for the Origin of Religion*. Chicago: University of Chicago Press, 1994.

———. *The Invention of World Religions: Or, How European Universalism Was Preserved in the Language of Pluralism*. Chicago: University of Chicago Press, 2005.

McKeown, Elizabeth. "After the Fall: Roman Catholic Modernism at the American Academy of Religion." *U.S. Catholic Historian* 20.3 (2002) 111–31.

McPheeters, W. M. "The Question of the Authorship of the Books of Scripture: A Criticism of Current Views." *Princeton Theological Review* 1 (1903) 362–83.

———. "The Question of Authorship: Practice versus Theory." *Princeton Theological Review* 1 (1903) 579–96.

Mettepenningen, Jürgen. *Nouvelle Théologie—New Theology: Inheritor of Modernism, Precursor of Vatican II*. London: T. & T. Clark, 2010.

Mettepenningen, Jürgen, and Ward De Pril. "Via media devenue précurseur en théologie: la 'troisième voie' entre modernisme et antimodernisme: Ambroise Gardeil et Léonce de Grandmaison." In *Science, Religion and Politics during the Modernist Crisis/Science, Religion et Politique à l'époque de la Crise Moderniste*, edited by Danny Praet and Corinne Bonnet, 251–77. Institut Historique Belge de Rome Études 5. Brussels and Rome: Istituto Storico Belga di Roma, 2018.

Milbank, John. *Theology and Social Theory: Beyond Secular Reason*. 2nd ed. Oxford: Blackwell, 2006 (1990).

Millard, A. R. "Aramaic in Nebuchadnezzar's Babylon." In *Recording New Epigraphic Evidence: Essays in Honor of Robert Deutsch*, edited by M. Lubetski and E. Lubetski, 113–21. Jerusalem: Leshon Limudim, 2015.

———. "Are There Anachronisms in the Books of Samuel?" In *Studies on the Text and Versions of the Hebrew Bible in Honour of Robert Gordon*, edited by G. Khan and D. Lipton, 39–48. Vetus Testamentum Supplements 149. Leiden: Brill, 2012.

———. "Assessing Solomon: History or Legend?" In *The Age of Solomon*, edited by L. K. Handy, 25–29. Studies in the History and Culture of the Ancient Near East 11. Leiden: Brill, 1997.

———. "Assyrian Royal Names in Biblical Hebrew." *Journal of Semitic Studies* 21 (1976) 1–14.

———. "Assyrians, Aramaeans and Aramaic." In *Homeland and Exile: Biblical and Ancient Near Eastern Studies in Honour of Bustenay Oded*, edited by G. Galil et al., 203–14. Vetus Testamentum Supplements 130. Leiden: Brill, 2009.

———. "Daniel in Babylon: An Accurate Record?" In *Do Historical Matters Matter?*, edited by James K. Hoffmeier and D. R. Magary, 263–80. Wheaton, IL: Crossway, 2012.

———. "Daniel 1–6 and History." *Evangelical Quarterly* 49 (1977) 67–73.

———. "David and Solomon's Jerusalem: Do the Bible and Archaeology Disagree?" In *Israel—Ancient Kingdom or Late Invention?*, edited by Daniel I. Block, 185–200. Nashville: B&H Academic, 2008.

———. "Deuteronomy and Ancient Hebrew History Writing in Light of Ancient Chronicles and Treaties." In *For Our Good Always: Studies on the Message and Influence of Deuteronomy in Honor of Daniel I. Block*, edited by J.S. DeRouchie et al., 3–15. Winona Lake, IN: Eisenbrauns, 2013.

———. "Donald John Wiseman, 1918–2010." *Proceedings of the British Academy* 172 (2011) 379–93.

———. "Hebrew Seals, Stamps and Statistic: How Can Fakes Be Found?" In *New Inscriptions and Seals Relating to the Biblical World*, edited by Meir Lubetski and Edith Lubetski, 183–91. Atlanta: Society of Biblical Literature, 2012.

———. "History and Legend in Early Babylonia." In *Windows into Old Testament History*, edited by V. Philips Long et al., 103–10. Grand Rapids: Eerdmans, 2002.

———. "How Reliable is Exodus?" *Biblical Archaeology Review* 26.4 (2000) 50–57.

———. "Israelite and Aramean History in the Light of Inscriptions." *Tyndale Bulletin* 41 (1990) 261–95.

———. "King Solomon in His Ancient Context." In *The Age of Solomon*, edited by L. K. Handy, 30–53. Studies in the History and Culture of the Ancient Near East 11. Leiden: Brill, 1997.

———. "The Knowledge of Writing in Late Bronze Age Palestine." In *Languages and Cultures in Contact: At the Crossroads of Civilizations in the Syro-Mesopotamian Realm*, edited by K. van Lerberghe and G. Voet, 317–26. Leuven: Peeters, 1999.

———. "Mesopotamia and the Bible." *Aram* 1 (1989) 24–30.

———. "Methods of Studying the Patriarchal Narratives as Ancient Texts." In *Essays on the Patriarchal Narratives*, edited by A. R. Millard and D. J. Wiseman, 43–58. Downers Grove, IL: InterVarsity, 1980.

———. "A New Babylonian 'Genesis' Story?" *Tyndale Bulletin* 18 (1967) 3–18.

———. "Owners and Users of Hebrew Seals." In *Frank Moore Cross Volume*, edited by Baruch A. Levine, 129–33. Jerusalem: Israel Exploration Society, 1999.

———. "Persian Names in Esther and the Reliability of the Hebrew Text." *Journal of Biblical Literature* 96 (1977) 481–88.

———. "The Practice of Writing in Ancient Israel." *Biblical Archaeologist* 35 (1972) 98–111.

———. "Ramesses Was Here . . . and Others Too!" In *Ramesside Studies in Honour of K.A. Kitchen*, edited by M. Collier and S. Snape, 305–12. Bolton: Rutherford, 2011.

———. *Reading and Writing in the Time of Jesus*. Sheffield: Sheffield Academic, 2000.

———. "Recently Discovered Hebrew Inscriptions." *Tyndale Bulletin* 11 (1962) 4–10.

———. "The Sign of the Flood." *Iraq* 49 (1987) 63–69.

———. "A Statue from Syria with Assyrian and Aramaic Inscriptions." *Biblical Archaeologist* 45 (1982) 135–41.

———. "Story, History and Theology." In *Faith, Tradition, and History: Old Testament Historiography in Its Near Eastern Context*, edited by A. R. Millard et al., 37–64. Winona Lake, IN: Eisenbrauns, 1994.

———. "The Tablets in the Ark." In *Reading the Law: Studies in Honour of Gordon J. Wenham*, edited by J. G. McConville, 254–66. London: T. & T. Clark, 2007.

———. "The Text of the Old Testament." In *A Bible Commentary for Today*, 27–39. London: Pickering & Inglis, 1979.

———. "Texts and Archaeology, Weighing the Evidence: The Case for King Solomon." *Palestinian Exploration Quarterly* 125 (1991) 19–27.

———. "The Value and Limitations of the Bible and Archaeology for Understanding the History of Israel—Some Examples." In *The Future of Biblical Archaeology*, edited by James K. Hoffmeier and A. R. Millard, 9–24. Grand Rapids: Eerdmans, 2004.

———. "A Wandering Aramean." *Journal of Near Eastern Studies* 39 (1980) 153–55.

———. "Were the Israelites Really Canaanites?" In *Israel—Ancient Kingdom or Late Invention?*, edited by Daniel I. Block, 156–68. Nashville: B&H Academic, 2008.

Miller, Glenn T. "The Pedagogy of Religion: A Study in the Thought of Joseph Kitagawa." *Perspectives in Religious Studies* 17.2 (1990) 117–27.

"Il modernismo: A rispetto della Chiesa." *La Civiltà cattolica* 4 (1883) 539–48.

Molendijk, Arie L. *Friedrich Max Müller and the Sacred Books of the East*. Oxford: Oxford University Press, 2016.

Montagnes, Bernard. *Le Père Lagrange (1855–1938): L'exégèse catholique dans la crise moderniste*. Paris: Cerf, 1995.

Morrison, Martha A. "A Continuing Adventure: Cyrus Gordon and Mesopotamia." *Biblical Archaeologist* 59 (1996) 31–35.

Morrow, Jeffrey L. "The Acid of History: La Peyrère, Hobbes, Spinoza, and the Separation of Faith and Reason in Modern Biblical Studies." *Heythrop Journal* 58 (2017) 169–80.

———. "Alfred Loisy's Developmental Approach to Scripture: Reading the 'Firmin' Articles in the Context of Nineteenth- and Twentieth-Century Historical Biblical Criticism." *International Journal of Systematic Theology* 15 (2013) 324–44.

———. *Alfred Loisy and Modern Biblical Studies*. Washington, DC: Catholic University of America Press, 2019.

———. "Alfred Loisy and les Mythes Babyloniens: Loisy's Discourse on Myth in the Context of Modernism." *Journal for the History of Modern Theology/ Zeitschrift für Neuere Theologiegeschichte* 21 (2014) 87–103.

———. "Alfred Loisy's Use of St. John Henry Newman: Newman's Contested Modernist Legacy." *Newman Studies Journal* 20.2 (2023) 68–84.

———. "Babylon in Paris: Alfred Loisy as Assyriologist." *Journal of Religious History* 40 (2016) 261–76.

———. "The Bible in Captivity: Hobbes, Spinoza and the politics of Defining Religion." *Pro Ecclesia* 19 (2010) 285–99.

———. "The Early Modern Political Context to Spinoza's Bible Criticism." *Revista de Filosofía* 66.3 (2010) 7–24.

———. "Edwin M. Yamauchi (1937–)." In *The Encyclopedia of Christian Literature Volumes 1–2*, edited by George Thomas Kurian and James D. Smith III, 653–54. Lanham, MD: Scarecrow, 2010.

———. "Études Bibliques: The Early Biblical Work of Alfred Loisy." *Modernism* 4 (2018) 12–32.

———. "Faith, Reason and History in Early Modern Catholic Biblical Interpretation: Fr. Richard Simon and St. Thomas More." *New Blackfriars* 96.1066 (2015) 658–73.

———. "The Fate of Catholic Biblical Interpretation in America." In *Weaving the American Catholic Tapestry: Essays in Honor of William L. Portier*, edited by Derek C. Hatch and Timothy R. Gabrielli, 41–59. Eugene, OR: Pickwick Publications, 2017.

———. "French Apocalyptic Messianism: Isaac La Peyrère and Political Biblical Criticism in the Seventeenth Century." *Toronto Journal of Theology* 27 (2011) 203–13.

———. "The 'Great Love Affair' with God." *Chesterton Review* 48 (2022) 429–38.

———. "*Leviathan* and the Swallowing of Scripture: The Politics behind Thomas Hobbes' Early Modern Biblical Criticism." *Christianity & Literature* 61.1 (2011) 33–54.

———. "Methods of Interpreting Scripture and Nature: The Influence of the Baconian Method on Spinoza's Bible Criticism." In *Studies in the History of Exegesis*, edited by Mark W. Elliott, Raleigh C. Heth, and Angela Zautcke, 157–73. Tübingen: Mohr Siebeck, 2022.

———. "Once There Was No Church and State: Re-Envisioning the Social Order in Light of Thirteenth Century History." *Nova et Vetera* 18 (2020) 991–1015.

———. "Pre-Adamites, Politics and Criticism: Isaac La Peyrère's Contribution to Modern Biblical Studies." *Journal of the Orthodox Center for the Advancement of Biblical Studies* 4.1 (2011) 1–23.

———. *Pretensions of Objectivity: Toward a Criticism of Biblical Criticism*. Eugene, OR: Pickwick Publications, 2019.

———. "Religion and the Secular State: Loisy's Use of 'Religion' Prior to His Excommunication." In *Constructing Nineteenth-Century Religion: Literary, Historical, and Religious Studies in Dialogue*, edited by Joshua King and Winter Jade Werner, 25–45. Columbus: Ohio State University Press 2019.

———. "The Reluctant Conversion of a Skeptic." In *By Strange Ways: Theologians and Their Paths to the Catholic Church*, edited by Jonathan Fuqua and Daniel Strudwick, 161–92. San Francisco: Ignatius, 2022.

———. Review of *Alfred Loisy and the Making of History of Religion: A Study of the Development of Comparative Religion in the Early 20th Century*, by Annelies Lannoy. *Theological Studies* 83 (2022) 160–61.

———. Review of *Science, Religion and Politics during the Modernist Crisis/ Science, Religion et Politique à l'époque de la Crise Moderniste*, edited by Danny Praet and Corinne Bonnet. *Heythrop Journal* 62 (2021) 130–32.

———. "75 Years of Comparative Religion at Miami University." *Ohio Academy of Religion Scholarly Papers* (2003) 81–87.

———. "Spinoza and the Theo-Political Implications of his Freedom to Philosophize." *New Blackfriars* 99 (2018) 374–87.

———. "Spinoza's Use of the Psalms in the Context of His Political Project." *Interdisciplinary Journal of Research on Religion* 11 (2015) 1–18.

———. *Theology, Politics, and Exegesis: Essays on the History of Modern Biblical Criticism*. Eugene, OR: Pickwick Publications, 2017.

———. *Three Skeptics and the Bible: La Peyrère, Hobbes, Spinoza, and the Reception of Modern Biblical Criticism*. Eugene, OR: Pickwick Publications, 2016.

———. "Thy Kingdom Come: The Church and the Kingdom of God in Loisy's *L'Évangile et l'Église*." *Downside Review* 137 (2019) 3–13.

———. "Yamauchi, Edwin Masao (b. 1937)." In *The Encyclopedia of Christian Civilization*, edited by George Thomas Kurian, Volume IV: S–Z, 2549–50. Oxford: Wiley-Blackwell, 2011.

Murphy, Roland E. "Historical Criticism." *Commonweal* (27 February 1998) 4 and 29.

———. "What Is Catholic About Catholic Biblical Scholarship?—Revisited." *Biblical Theology Bulletin* 28 (1998) 112–19.

Nelson, Eric. *The Hebrew Republic: Jewish Sources and the Transformation of European Political Thought*. Cambridge: Harvard University Press, 2010.

Nongbri, Brent. *Before Religion: A History of a Modern Concept*. New Haven: Yale University Press, 2013.

O'Connell, Marvin R. "The Bishopric of Monaco, 1902: A Revision." *Catholic Historical Review* 71 (1985) 26–51.

———. *Critics on Trial: An Introduction to the Catholic Modernist Crisis*. Washington, DC: Catholic University of America Press, 1994.

Petráček, Tomáš. *The Bible and the Crisis of Modernism: Catholic Criticism in the Twentieth Century*. Notre Dame, IN: University of Notre Dame Press, 2022.

Petre, M. D. *Alfred Loisy: His Religious Significance*. Cambridge: Cambridge University Press, 1944.

Pitre, Brant. *Jesus and the Last Supper*. Grand Rapids: Eerdmans, 2015.

———. *Jesus, the Tribulation, and the End of the Exile: Restoration Eschatology and the Origin of the Atonement*. Tübingen: Mohr Siebeck, 2005.

Portier, William L. *Divided Friends: Portraits of the Roman Catholic Modernist Crisis in the United States*. Washington, DC: The Catholic University of America Press, 2013.

---. "Fundamentalism in North America: A Modern Anti-Modernism." *Communio* 28 (2001) 581–98.

---. "Here Come the Evangelical Catholics." *Communio* 31 (2004) 35–66.

---. "Jesus and the World of Grace, 1968–2016: An Idiosyncratic Theological Memoir." *Horizons* 43 (2016) 374–96.

---. Preface to *Modernists & Mystics*, edited by C. J. T. Talar, ix–xi. Washington, DC: Catholic University of America Press, 2009.

---. "Thomist Resurgence." *Communio* 35 (2008) 494–504.

Poulat, Émile. *Histoire, dogme, et critique dans la crise moderniste*. Paris: Casterman, 1962.

Praet, Danny. "L'affaire Cumon. Idéologies et politique académique à l'université de Gand au cours de la crise moderniste." In *Science, Religion and Politics during the Modernist Crisis/Science, Religion et Politique à l'époque de la Crise Moderniste*, edited by Danny Praet and Corinne Bonnet, 339–402. Institut Historique Belge de Rome Études 5. Brussels and Rome: Istituto Storico Belga di Roma, 2018.

---. "Symbolisme, évolution rituelle et morale dans l'histoire des religions: le cas du *Taurobolium* dans les publications et la correspondance de Franz Cumont et d'Alfred Loisy." *Mythos* 7 (2013) 127–45.

Praet, Danny and Annelies Lannoy. "Alfred Loisy's Comparative Method in *Les mystères païens et le mystère chrétien*." *Numen* 64 (2017) 64–96.

Praet, Danny and Corinne Bonnet. Introduction to *Science, Religion and Politics during the Modernist Crisis/Science, Religion et Politique à l'époque de la Crise Moderniste*, edited by Danny Praet and Corinne Bonnet, VII–XXXII. Institut Historique Belge de Rome Études 5. Brussels and Rome: Istituto Storico Belga di Roma, 2018.

---, ed. *Science, Religion and Politics during the Modernist Crisis/Science, Religion et Politique à l'époque de la Crise Moderniste*. Institut Historique Belge de Rome Études 5. Brussels and Rome: Istituto Storico Belga di Roma, 2018.

Priest, Robert D. *The Gospel According to Renan: Reading, Writing, and Religion in Nineteenth-Century France*. Oxford: Oxford University Press, 2015.

Ratzinger, Joseph Cardinal. *Called to Communion: Understanding the Church Today*. San Francisco: Ignatius, 1996 (1991).

---. *Jesus of Nazareth: From the Baptism in the Jordan to the Transfiguration*. New York: Doubleday, 2007.

Reinach, Salomon. *Orpheus. Histoire générale des religions*. Paris: Picard, 1907.

Renan, Ernest. *Histoire du peuple d'Israël Tome 5*. Paris: Calmann Lévy, 1893.

Rendsburg, Gary A. "Cyrus H. Gordon (1908–2001): A Giant Among Scholars." *Jewish Quarterly Review* 92 (2001) 137–43.

---. "'Someone Will Succeed in Deciphering Minoan': Cyrus H. Gordon and Minoan Linear A." *Biblical Archaeologist* 59 (1996) 36–43.

Resch, Richard. "History and Dogma and Individual Psychology." *Journal of Religion* 59 (1979) 35–55.

BIBLIOGRAPHY

Reynolds, Frank E., and Theodore M. Ludwig. "Joseph Mitsuo Kitagawa—Biographical Sketch, Activities and Bibliography." In *Transitions and Transformations in the History of Religions: Essays in Honor of Joseph M. Kitagawa*, edited by Frank E. Reynolds and Theodore M. Ludwig, 1–11. Leiden: Brill, 1980.

Ricketts, Mac Linscott. "Mircea Eliade: Biographical Note." In *Mircea Eliade: Myth, Religion, and History*, edited by Nicolae Babuts, xi–xiv. New York: Routledge, 2014.

Schelkens, Karim. "'Le plus aristocratique des goûts'. Modernist, Orientalist and Anti-Semitic Bible Readings in Late 19th-Century Belgium." In *Science, Religion and Politics during the Modernist Crisis/Science, Religion et Politique à l'époque de la Crise Moderniste*, edited by Danny Praet and Corinne Bonnet, 193–220. Institut Historique Belge de Rome Études 5. Brussels and Rome: Istituto Storico Belga di Roma, 2018.

Schönborn, Christoph Cardinal, OP. "The Kingdom of God and the Heavenly-Earthly Church." *Letter & Spirit* 2 (2006) 217–34.

———. "Il significativo ecclesiologico del Concilio Ecumenico Vaticano II." In *Realizzare il Concilio. Il contributo di Communione e Liberazione*, 23. Milan: Litterae communionis, 1982.

Schreiber, Jean-Philippe. "Eugène Goblet d'Alviella et les réactions catholiques à son étude scientifique de la religion (1884–1886)." In *Science, Religion and Politics during the Modernist Crisis/Science, Religion et Politique à l'époque de la Crise Moderniste*, edited by Danny Praet and Corinne Bonnet, 281–321. Institut Historique Belge de Rome Études 5. Brussels and Rome: Istituto Storico Belga di Roma, 2018.

Schultenover, David G., SJ. *Jesuit Superior General Luis Martín García and His Memorias: "Showing Up"*. Jesuit Studies 30. Leiden: Brill, 2021.

Segal, Robert A. "Eliade on Myth and Science." In *Mircea Eliade: Myth, Religion, and History*, edited by Nicolae Babuts, 65–76. New York: Routledge, 2014.

———. "William Robertson Smith vis-à-vis Émile Durkheim as Sociologist of Religion." *Journal of Scottish Thought* 1.2 (2008) 1–12.

Smith, Jonathan Z. "The Eternal Deferral." In *Hermeneutics, Politics, and the History of Religions: The Contested Legacies of Joachim Wach and Mircea Eliade*, edited by Christian K. Wedemeyer and Wendy Doniger, 215–39. Oxford: Oxford University Press, 2010.

Supreme Sacred Congregation of the Holy Office and the Universal Inquisition. "Quo sub 65 propositionibus reprobantur ac proscribuntur praecipui errores reformismi seu modernism." [*Lamentabili sane exitu*] *Acta Sanctae Sedis* 40 (1907) 470–78.

Talar, C. J. T. "Between Science and Myth: Alfred Loisy on Genesis." *Mythos* 7 (2013) 27–41.

———. "The French Connection: The Church's 'Eldest Daughter' and the Condemnation of Modernism." *U.S. Catholic Historian* 25 (2007) 55–69.

———. "Innovation and Biblical Interpretation." In *Catholicism Contending with Modernity: Roman Catholic Modernism and Anti-Modernism in Historical Context*, edited by Darrell Jodock, 191–211. Cambridge: Cambridge University Press, 2000.

———. *Metaphor and Modernist: The Polarization of Alfred Loisy and His Neo-Thomist Critics*. Lanham: University Press of America, 1987.

———. "A Reading of the Gospel (and the Church) According to Alfred Loisy." *Thought* 67 (1992) 302–16.

———. *(Re)reading, Reception, and Rhetoric: Approaches to Roman Catholic Modernism*. New York: Lang, 1999.

———. "Salomon Reinach's *Orpheus*: Catalyst for Debate over the History of Religions in France." In *Science, Religion and Politics during the Modernist Crisis/Science, Religion et Politique à l'époque de la Crise Moderniste*, editd by Danny Praet and Corinne Bonnet, 49–71. Institut Historique Belge de Rome Études 5. Brussels and Rome: Istituto Storico Belga di Roma, 2018.

Tanner, Norman P., SJ., ed. *Decrees of the Ecumenical Councils Volume Two: Trent to Vatican II*. Washington, DC: Georgetown University Press, 1990.

Taylor, Charles. *A Secular Age*. Cambridge: Harvard University Press, 2007.

Théobald, Christoph. "L'Exégèse catholique au moment de la crise moderniste." In *Le Monde contemporain et la Bible*, edited by Claude Savart and Jean-Noël Aletti, 387–439. Paris: Beauchesne, 1985.

Thompson, Thomas L. *The Historicity of the Patriarchal Narratives: The Quest for the Historical Abraham*. Berlin: de Gruyter, 1974.

Toupin-Guyot, Claire. "L'intellectuel catholique ou l'intrusion du regard étranger?" In *Science, Religion and Politics during the Modernist Crisis/ Science, Religion et Politique à l'époque de la Crise Moderniste*, edited by Danny Praet and Corinne Bonnet, 99–115. Institut Historique Belge de Rome Études 5. Brussels and Rome: Istituto Storico Belga di Roma, 2018.

Trémolières, François. "Au confluent de l'étude scientifique de la mystique et de la controverse anti-moderniste: la notion d'expérience." In *Science, Religion and Politics during the Modernist Crisis/Science, Religion et Politique à l'époque de la Crise Moderniste*, edited by Danny Praet and Corinne Bonnet, 73–98. Institut Historique Belge de Rome Études 5. Brussels and Rome: Istituto Storico Belga di Roma, 2018.

Tsumura, David Toshio. "The Father of Ugaritic Studies." *Biblical Archaeologist* 59 (1996) 44–50.

Turvasi, Francesco. *The Condemnation of Alfred Loisy and the Historical Method*. Rome: Edizioni di Storia e Letteratura, 1979.

Wernz, W. J. "Loisy's 'Modernist' Writings." *Downside Review* 92 (1974) 25–45.

Wilson, R. D. "The Use of 'God' and 'Lord' in the Koran." *Princeton Theological Review* 17 (1919) 644–50.

Wineland, John D. Preface to *The Light of Discovery: Studies in Honor of Edwin M. Yamauchi*, edited by John D. Wineland, xv–xvii. Eugene, OR: Pickwick Publications, 2007.

BIBLIOGRAPHY

Wiseman, D. J. "Abraham in History and Tradition: Abraham the Hebrew: Part 1." *Bibliotheca Sacra* 134 (1977) 123–30.

———. "Abraham in History and Tradition: Abraham the Prince: Part 2." *Bibliotheca Sacra* 134 (1977) 228–37.

———. "Abraham Reassessed." In *Essays on the Patriarchal Narratives*, edited by A.R. Millard and D. J. Wiseman, 141–60. Downers Grove, IL: InterVarsity, 1980.

———. "Archaeological Confirmation of the Old Testament." In *Revelation and the Bible: Contemporary Evangelical Thought*, edited by Carl F. H. Henry, 301–16. London: Tyndale House, 1959.

———. "Archaeology and Scripture." *Westminster Theological Journal* 33 (1971) 133–52.

———. *The Cambridge Ancient History: Assyria and Babylonia c. 1200–1000 B.C.: Revised Edition of Volumes I & II*. Cambridge: Cambridge University Press, 1965.

———. *1 and 2 Kings: An Introduction and Commentary*. London: Tyndale House, 1993.

———. "'Is It Peace?': Covenant and Diplomacy." *Vetus Testamentum* 32 (1982) 311–26.

———. "Jonah's Nineveh." *Tyndale Bulletin* 30 (1979) 29–52.

———. *Life Above and Below*. Self-published: 2003.

———. *Nebuchadrezzar and Babylon*. Oxford: Oxford University Press, 1983.

———. "Rahab of Jericho." *Tyndale Bulletin* 14 (1964) 8–11.

———. "Some Historical Problems in the Book of Daniel." In *Notes on Some Problems in the Book of Daniel*, edited by D. J. Wiseman, 9–18. London: Tyndale House, 1965.

Wiseman, Donald J., and Edwin M. Yamauchi. *Archaeology and the Bible*. Grand Rapids: Zondervan, 1979.

Wolf, Hubert and Judith Schepers, eds. *"In wilder zügelloser Jagd nach Neuem": 100 Jahre Modernismus und Antimodernismus in der katholischen Kirche*. Paderborn: Schöningh, 2010.

Yamauchi, Edwin M. "The Achaemenid Capitals." *Near Eastern Archaeological Society Bulletin* 8 (1976) 5–81.

———. "Ahasuerus." In *The Anchor Bible Dictionary Volume 1*, ed. David Noel Freedman, 105. New York: Doubleday, 1992.

———. "An Ancient Historian's View of Christianity." In *Professors Who Believe: The Spiritual Journeys of Christian Faculty*, ed. Paul M. Anderson, 192–99. Downers Grove, IL: InterVarsity, 1998.

———. "The Apocalypse of Adam, Mithraism and Pre-Christian Gnosticism." In *Études Mithraiques, Textes et Mémoires*, edited by Duchesne-Guillemin, 537–63. Teheran: Bibliothèque Pahlavi, 1978.

———. "Aramaic Magic Bowls." *Journal of the American Oriental Society* 85 (1965) 511–23.

———. "The Archaeological Background of Daniel." In *Vital Old Testament Issues*, ed. Roy B. Zuck, 160–70. Grand Rapids: Kregel, 1996.

———. "The Archaeological Background of Esther." *Bibliotheca Sacra* 137 (1980) 99–117.

———. "The Archaeological Background of Ezra." *Bibliotheca Sacra* 137 (1980) 195–211.

———. "The Archaeological Background of Nehemiah." *Bibliotheca Sacra* 137 (1980) 291–309.

———. "The Archaeological Confirmation of Suspect Elements in the Classical and the Biblical Traditions." In *The Law and the Prophets*, ed. J. Skilton, 54–70. Nutley, NJ: Presbyterian & Reformed, 1974.

———. "Archaeology and the Bible." In *The Oxford Companion to the Bible*, edited by Bruce M. Metzger and Michael D. Coogan, 46–54. Oxford: Oxford University Press, 1993.

———. "The Archaeology of Biblical Africa: Cyrene in Libya." *Archaeology in the Biblical World* 2 (1992) 6–18.

———. "Archaeology and the Gospels: Discoveries and Publications of the Past Decade (1977–1987)." In *The Gospels Today*, edited by J. H. Skilton, 1–12. Philadelphia: Skilton House, 1990.

———. "Archaeology and the New Testament." In *The Expositor's Bible Commentary*, ed. F. E. Gaebelein, 645–69. Grand Rapids: Zondervan, 1979.

———. *The Archaeology of New Testament Cities in Western Asia Minor*. Grand Rapids: Baker Book House, 1980.

———. *An Asian American Ancient Historian and Biblical Scholar*. Eugene, OR: Resource Publications, 2024.

———. *Composition and Corroboration in Classical and Biblical Studies*. Philadelphia: Presbyterian & Reformed, 1966.

———. "The Current State of Old Testament Historiography." In *Faith, Tradition, and History: Old Testament Historiography in Its Near Eastern Context*, edited by A. sR. Millard, James K. Hoffmeier, and David W. Baker, 1–36. Winona Lake: Eisenbrauns, 1994.

———. "Daniel and Contacts between the Aegean and the Near East before Alexander." *Evangelical Quarterly* 53 (1981) 37–47.

———. "Darius the Persian." In *Wycliffe Bible Encyclopedia*, edited by C. F. Pfeiffer, et al., 425. Chicago: Moody, 1975.

———. "A Decade and a Half of Archaeology in Israel and in Jordan." *Journal of the American Academy of Religion* 42 (1974) 710–26.

———. "The Descent of Ishtar, the Fall of Sophia, and the Jewish Roots of Gnosticism." *Tyndale Bulletin* 29 (1978) 140–71.

———. "Did Christianity Copy Earlier Pagan Resurrection Stories?" In *The Harvest Handbook of Apologetics*, edited by Joseph M. Holden, 149–56. Eugene, OR: Harvest House, 2018.

———. "Did Persian Zoroastrianism Influence Judaism?" In *Israel: Ancient Kingdom or Late Invention?*, ed. Daniel I. Block, 282–97. Nashville: B&H Academic, 2008.

———. "Documents from Old Testament Times." *Westminster Theological Journal* 41 (1978) 1-32.

———. "Easter: Myth, Hallucination, or History?" *Christianity Today* 18 (15 March and 29 March 1974) 4-7, 12-14, and 16.

———. "Elchasaites, Manichaeans and Mandaeans in the Light of the Cologne Mani Codex." In *Beyond the Jordan: Studies in Honor of W. Harold Mare*, ed. Glenn A. Carnagey, 49-60. Eugene, OR: Wipf & Stock, 2005.

———. "The Episode of the Magi." In *Chronos, Kairos, Christos: Nativity and Chronological Studies Presented to Jack Finegan*, ed. Jerry Vardaman and Edwin M. Yamauchi, 15-39. Winona Lake, IN: Eisenbrauns, 1989.

———. "Ezra and Nehemiah." In *Zondervan Illustrated Bible Backgrounds Commentary*, ed. John H. Walton, 394-467. Grand Rapids: Zondervan, 2009.

———. *Foes from the Northern Frontier*. Grand Rapids: Baker Book House, 1982.

———. *Gnostic Ethics and Mandaean Origins*. Cambridge: Harvard University Press, 1970.

———. "Gnosticism and Early Christianity." In *Hellenization Revisited*, ed. W. Helleman, 29-61. Lanham, MD: University Press of America, 1994.

———. "The Gnostics and History." *Journal of the Evangelical Theological Society* 14 (1971) 29-40.

———. "'God and the Shah': Church and State in Sasanid Persia." *Fides et Historia* 30 (1998) 80-99.

———. *Greece and Babylon: Early Contacts between the Aegean and the Near East*. Grand Rapids: Baker, 1967.

———. "The Greek Words in Daniel in the Light of Greek Influence in the Near East." In *New Perspectives on the Old Testament*, edited by J. B. Payne, 170-200. Waco, TX: Word, 1970.

———. "Hermeneutical Issues in the Book of Daniel." *Journal of the Evangelical Theological Society* 23 (1980) 13-21.

———. "Historical Notes on the (In)comparable Christ." *Christianity Today* 16 (22 October 1971) 7-11.

———. "Historical Notes on the Trial and Crucifixion of Jesus Christ." *Christianity Today* 15 (9 April 1971) 6-11.

———. "The Issue of Pre-Christian Gnosticism Reviewed in the Light of the Nag Hammadi Texts." In *The Nag Hammadi Library after Fifty Years*, edited by John Turner and Anne McGuire, 72-88. Nag Hammadi and Manichaean Studies 44. Leiden: Brill, 1997.

———. "Jesus Outside the New Testament: What is the Evidence?" In *Jesus Under Fire*, edited by Michael J. Wilkins and J. P. Moreland, 207-29. Grand Rapids: Zondervan, 1995.

———. "Jewish Gnosticism? The Prologue of John, Mandaean Parallels, and the Trimorphic Protennoia." In *Studies in Gnosticism and Hellenistic Religions*, edited by R. Van Den Broek and M. J. Vermaseren, 467-97. Etudes préliminaires aux religions orientales dans l'Empire romain 91. Leiden: Brill, 1981.

———. "Life, Death, and the Afterlife in the Ancient Near East." In *Life in the Face of Death: The Resurrection Message of the New Testament*, edited by Richard N. Longenecker, 21–50. Grand Rapids: Eerdmans, 1998.

———. "Magic Bowls: Cyrus H. Gordon and the Ubiquity of Magic in the Pre-Modern World." *Biblical Archaeologist* 59 (1996) 51–55.

———. *Mandaic Incantation Texts*. New Haven: American Oriental Society, 1967.

———. "Mandaic Incantations: Lead Rolls and Magic Bowls." *Aram* 11–12 (1999–2000) 253–68.

———. "A Mandaic Magic Bowl from the Yale Babylonian Collection." *Berytus* 17 (1967) 49–63.

———. "Mandaeism." In *Supplementary Volume, The Interpreter's Dictionary of the Bible*, ed. K. Crim, 563. Nashville: Abingdon, 1976.

———. "A Model Leader: Leadership in Nehemiah." In *Biblical Leadership: Theology for the Everyday Leader*, ed. Benjamin R. Forrest and Chet Roden, 266–76. Grand Rapids: Kregel Academic, 2017.

———. "Mordecai, the Persepolis Tablets, and the Susa Excavations." *Vetus Testamentum* 42 (1992) 272–75.

———. "Nehemiah, a Model Leader." In *A Spectrum of Thought: Essays in Honor of Dennis F. Kinlaw*, ed. Michael L. Peterson, 171–80. Wilmore, KY: Francis Asbury, 1982.

———. "Notes on Ezra, Nehemiah, Esther." In *The NIV Study Bible*, ed. Kenneth Barker, 670–730. Grand Rapids: Zondervan, 1985.

———. "Obelisks and Pyramids." *Near Eastern Archaeological Society Bulletin* 24 (1985) 111–15.

———. *Persia and the Bible*. Grand Rapids: Baker, 1990.

———. "Persians." In *Peoples of the Old Testament World*, edited by Alfred J. Hoerth et al., 107–24. Grand Rapids: Baker, 1994.

———. "Post-Biblical Traditions about Ezra and Nehemiah." In *A Tribute to Gleason Archer*, ed. Walter Kaiser and Ronald Youngblood, 167–76. Chicago: Moody, 1986.

———. *Pre-Christian Gnosticism*. London: Tyndale, 1973.

———. "Pre-Christian Gnosticism in the Nag Hammadi Texts?" *Church History* 48 (1979) 129–41.

———. "The Present Status of Mandaean Studies." *Journal of Near Eastern Studies* 25 (1966) 88–96.

———. "Ramsay's Views on Archaeology in Asia Minor Reviewed." In *The New Testament Student and His Field*, ed. J.H. Skilton and C. A. Ladley, 27–40. Phillipsburg, NJ: Presbyterian & Reformed, 1982.

———. "Recent Archaeological Work in the New Testament Cities of Western Anatolia." *Near Eastern Archaeological Society Bulletin* 13 (1979) 37–116.

———. "The Reconstruction of Jewish Communities During the Persian Empire." In *Tough-Minded Christianity: Honoring the Legacy of John W. Montgomery*, edited by William Dembski and Thomas Shirrmacher, 350–74. Nashville: B&H Academic, 2008.

———. "Religions of the Biblical World: Persia." In *The International Standard Bible Encyclopedia*, edited by G.W. Bromiley, 123–29. Grand Rapids: Eerdmans, 1988.

———. "The Reverse Order of Ezra/Nehemiah Reconsidered." *Themelios* 5.3 (1980) 7–13.

———. *The Scriptures and Archaeology*. Portland, OR: Western Conservative Baptist Seminary, 1980.

———. "The Scythians: Invading Hordes from the Russian Steppes." *Biblical Archaeologist* 46 (1983) 90–99.

———. "Some Alleged Evidence for Pre-Christian Gnosticism." In *New Dimensions in New Testament Studies*, edited by Richard N. Longenecker and M. Tenney, 46–70. Grand Rapids: Zondervan, 1975.

———. *The Stones and the Scriptures*. Philadelphia: Lippincott, 1972.

———. "Susa." In *The New International Dictionary of Biblical Archaeology*, ed. E. M. Blaiklock and R. K. Harrison, 426–30. Grand Rapids: Zondervan, 1983.

———. "Two Reformers Compared: Solon of Athens and Nehemiah of Jerusalem." In *The Bible World: Essays in Honor of Cyrus H. Gordon*, edited by Gary Rendsburg et al., 269–92. New York: Ktav, 1980.

———. "Vashti." In *Dictionary of the Old Testament: Wisdom, Poetry & Writings*, ed. Tremper Longmann III and Peter Enns, 825–28. Downers Grove, IL: IVP Academic, 2008.

———. "Was Nehemiah the Cupbearer a Eunuch?" *Zeitschrift für die alttestamentliche Wissenschaft* 92 (1980) 132–42.

Zambarbieri, Annibale. "Anesaki Masaharu (1873–1949) in Italia «au cœur de la crise moderniste»." In *Science, Religion and Politics during the Modernist Crisis/Science, Religion et Politique à l'époque de la Crise Moderniste*, ed. Danny Praet and Corinne Bonnet, 157–76. Institut Historique Belge de Rome Études 5. Brussels and Rome: Istituto Storico Belga di Roma, 2018.

Subject Index

Adorno, Theodor W., 13–14, 101
Albright, William Foxwell, 13
American Academy of Religion, 5–6, 21n66, 55n41
Amiaud, Arthur, 25
Assyriology, 10, 12, 13n31, 21–22, 25, 27, 43, 46, 51, 62, 70n50, 73–74, 76

Benedict XV, Pope, 2, 36
Benedict XVI, Pope/Joseph Ratzinger, 36, 80, 112
Blondel, Maurice, 33, 38, 92–93, 97

Comparative Religion, 7, 26, 34, 39–40, 42, 44, 48
Congar, Yves, 37–38, 98
Cumont, Franz, 26, 29, 33, 38, 40, 42, 44, 46, 54, 73n76, 86n28

Daniélou, Jean, 37
de Lubac, Henri, 37–38
Divino Afflante Spiritu, 15, 36
Documentary Hypothesis, 18, 19n61
Duchesne, Louis, 25, 61, 65n28, 82n10

Durkheim, Émile, 44–45, 48, 51–54

Egyptology, 10–12, 19n60, 62
Eliade, Mircea, 6, 8

Frankfurt School, 13–14
Frazer, James, 44, 48

Garrigou-Lagrange, Réginald, 32, 37
Gigot, François, 18–19, 100
Gordon, Cyrus H., 8, 11, 13, 100

Halévy, Joseph, 69n49, 70
Harnack, Adolf, 35, 46, 60, 65n28, 78, 82–83, 84n20, 85–88, 90, 100
histoire des religions, 38–39, 49, 51
History of Religion/s, 2, 24, 30–34, 41–49, 51, 56, 59, 73n76, 86n28
Hobbes, Thomas, 15–16
Horkheimer, Max, 13–14, 101

John XXIII, Pope St, 2

Kant, Immanuel, 31
Kitagawa, Joseph, 8, 44

SUBJECT INDEX

La Peyrère, Isaac, 16
La Société Internationale d'Études sur Alfred Loisy, 2-3, 5-6, 21, 44, 55
Lagrange, Marie-Joseph, 15, 17, 33, 38, 40, 58n4-5, 81, 93, 103
Lamentabili Sane Exitu, 57, 84, 94
Le Muséon, 36
Leo XIII, Pope, 1, 3, 15, 31, 59, 63, 76
L'Évangile et l'Église, 25, 43, 45-46, 55, 58-60, 78-79, 80n3-4, 81-88, 89n42-48, 90-92, 104
Loisy, Alfred, 1-3, 5, 7, 15-17, 19-27, 33-34, 37-38, 40-94, 104-6

MacIntyre, Alasdair, 14, 31-32n15, 35n24, 106
Marquise Arconati-Visconti, 47
Miami University, 7-8, 39, 44
Michaelis, Johann David, 17, 50
Müller, Friedrich Max, 34, 44-45, 49n22, 69n49

Newman, St. John Henry, 23, 46, 53
Nineteenth Century Theology Group, 6, 21n66
Nouvelle Théologie, 32, 37-38

Oppert, Jules, 21, 70

Pascendi Dominici Gregis, 1, 16, 18-19, 23-24, 29, 31-36, 38, 84n22, 93-94
Pius IX, Pope, 16, 36
Pius X, Pope St, 1, 16-17, 20, 23-24, 29, 31, 35-37, 57, 84n22, 94
Pius XII, Pope, 15, 36

Pontifical Biblical Commission, 16, 35
Providentissimus Deus, 1, 3, 15, 59, 63, 76

Reinach, Salomon, 30-32, 48, 112
Religionsgeschichte, 49, 51
Religionswissenschaft, 34
Renan, Ernest, 25, 49n22, 60-62, 65n28, 69n49, 70, 80n4, 82n10, 87, 88n38, 112
Reuss, Édouard, 25, 64-66, 71n64, 72, 80n4
Roman Catholic Modernism Group, 5-6

Science of Religion, 34, 46
Second Vatican Council, 3, 15, 33, 36, 38, 54-55, 59, 77-79, 80n2, 81, 91-93
Simon, Richard, 15-17, 22-23, 64, 65n28, 69n49, 75
Smith, William Robertson, 44-45
Sodalitium Pianum, 19, 36
Spinoza, Baruch, 15-17
Syllabus of Errors, 16, 36

Tylor, E.B., 44
Tyrrell, George, 34, 37-38, 93

University of Chicago, 7, 44

Vigouroux, Fulcran Grégoire, 17, 60-61, 69n49, 73
von Hügel, Friedrich, 53, 93

Wellhausen, Julius, 13, 18, 21-22, 45, 62, 69n49, 74

Yamauchi, Edwin M., 8-11, 13, 15, 19

Author Index

Adorno, Theodor W., 13-14, 101
Åkerman, Susanna, 47n16, 95
Aling, Charles F., 19, 95
Allen, Douglas, 8n7, 95
Arnold, Bill T., 35n26, 95-96
Arnold, Claus, 1n1, 2n2, 28n2, 57n1, 82n11, 84, 94n2, 94n4-6, 96
Art, Jan, 40, 96
Asad, Talal, 51n28, 96

Barber, Michael Patrick, 90n52, 96
Barmann, Lawrence F., 6n4, 58, 96-97
Bea, Augustin, 18, 97
Beidelman, T. O., 45n7, 97
Benedict XVI, Pope/Joseph Ratzinger, 36, 80, 112
Bergsma, John S., 62n18, 97
Bernardi, Peter J., 38n34, 97
Blanchette, Oliva, 38n34, 97
Block, Daniel I., 12n29, 97
Blondel, Maurice, 33, 38, 92-93, 97
Bonnet, Corinne, 2, 27n1, 28-30, 32, 35-36, 40-41, 43, 56, 97, 112
Botti, Alfonso, 28n5, 97

Boyd, J. O., 18n55, 97
Burke, Ronald, 24n69, 97

Calvert, Kenneth R., 8n10, 98
Carmignac, Jean, 80n4, 98
Cassuto, Umberto, 18, 98
Cavanaugh, William T., 14, 51n28, 98
Cerrato, Rocco, 28n5, 97
Chanel, Christian, 33-34, 98
Chen, Y.S., 62n17, 98
Ciappa, Rosanna, 92n64, 98
Colin, Pierre, 31n14, 98
Collins, John J., 65n24, 98
Congar, Yves, 37-38, 98
Courtois, Luc, 36, 98

Daly, Gabriel, 31n14, 82n12-13, 83n19, 98-99
D'Costa, Gavin, 14, 99
De Maeyer, Jan, 34, 99
De Pril, Ward, 37, 82n10, 99, 107
Dietrich, Wendell S., 8on3, 99

Ellwood, Robert S., 8n7, 99

Feil, Ernst, 51n28, 99

AUTHOR INDEX

Feldman, Louis H., 8n11, 99
Feller, Yaniv, 35n26, 99
Fogarty, Gerald P., 19n62, 99

Geyer, Carl-Friedrich, 81n7, 99
Gigot, François, 18–19, 100
Gillespie, Michael Allen, 50, 100
Ginzburg, Carlo, 8n7, 100
Gordon, Cyrus H., 8, 11, 13, 100
Gottlieb, Claire, 8n11, 106
Gregory, Brad S., 50n26, 100
Gross, Michael B., 52n31, 100

Hahn, Scott W., 16n48, 45n8, 52n33, 67n38, 100
Hallo, William W., 62n17, 100
Harnack, Adolf, 35, 46, 60, 65n28, 78, 82–83, 84n20, 85–88, 90, 100
Harrison, Peter, 51n28, 100
Hauerwas, Stanley, 14, 52, 100
Hill, Harvey, 6n4, 43n5, 48n18, 81n7, 82n12, 82n14, 82n16, 83n17, 85, 86n27, 91n57–59, 92, 97, 100
Hoffmeier, James K., 10–11, 13n30, 19, 101
Horkheimer, Max, 13–14, 101

Idel, Moshe, 8n7, 101
Israel, Jonathan I., 17n52, 101
Izquierdo, César, 38n34, 92n64, 101–2

Jacobs, Joseph Harry, 91n59, 102
Jodock, Darrell, 6n4, 102
Johnson, Luke Timothy, 15, 16n49, 102
Jones, Andrew Willard, 50, 102
Jung, Dietrich, 45n7, 102

Kaufmann, Yehezkel, 18, 102
Kenis, Leo, 29n7, 34, 99, 102
Kerr, Fergus, 31, 32n15, 102

Kirwan, Jon, 32n17, 37n32, 93n1, 102
Kitchen, Kenneth A., 10–11, 12n27, 102–3

Lagrange, Marie-Joseph, 15, 17, 33, 38, 40, 58n4–5, 81, 93, 103
Lahutsky, Nadia, 38n35, 58n5, 103
Lambert, W. G., 11n23, 103
Lannoy, Annelies, 2–3, 24n70, 28n2, 40–41, 43–49, 51, 52n30, 53–56, 59, 86n28, 103, 112
Laplanche, François, 24, 25n72, 60n12–13, 104
Legaspi, Michael C., 50, 104
Lehner, Ulrich L., 17, 50n26, 104
Lenormant, François, 69n49, 76, 104
Levenson, Jon D., 15, 104
Loisy, Alfred, 1–3, 5, 7, 15–17, 19–27, 33–34, 37–38, 40–94, 104–6
Losito, Giacomo, 29–30, 57n1, 82n11, 84n22, 94n2, 94n4–5, 96, 106
Lubetski, Meir, 8n11, 106
Ludwig, Theodore M., 8n8, 113

Machinist, Peter, 13n31, 21, 62n19, 106
MacIntyre, Alasdair, 14, 31–32n15, 35n24, 106
Maher, Anthony M., 28n2, 106
Maier, Bernhard, 45n7, 106
Maier, Paul L., 8n10, 106
Mansini, Guy, 31n14, 106
Marblestone, Howard, 8n11, 106
Marshner, William H., 28n2, 106
Maryanski, Alexandra, 45n7, 106
Masuzawa, Tomoko, 35, 49, 88n38, 106–7
McKeown, Elizabeth, 6n3, 107
McPheeters, W. M., 18n55, 107
Mettepenningen, Jürgen, 37, 93n1, 107

AUTHOR INDEX

Milbank, John, 8, 14–15, 32, 107
Millard, A.R., 10, 10–11n23, 12, 21, 103, 107–9
Miller, Glenn T., 8n8, 109
Molendijk, Arie L., 34n21, 109
Montagnes, Bernard, 58n4, 109
Morrison, Martha A., 8n11, 109
Morrow, Jeffrey L., 2n3, 2n5, 3n7–9, 5n1, 7n5–6, 8n10, 16n47–49, 25n73, 28n2, 39n37, 43n1, 43n5, 44n6, 45n8, 46n12, 47n13–14, 48n18, 50n27, 51n28, 52n33, 53n34, 53n36, 55n40, 56n42, 56n45, 57n2, 58n6, 59n8, 61n14, 62n16, 62n18, 67n38, 70n50, 94n3, 97, 100, 109–111
Murphy, Roland E., 15, 111

Nelson, Eric, 50n26, 111
Nongbri, Brent, 51n28, 111

O'Connell, Marvin R., 19, 81, 82–83n16, 111

Petráček, Tomáš, 28n2, 111
Petre, M. D., 91n59, 111
Pitre, Brant, 87n33, 89n48, 111
Portier, William L., 6n2–3, 7, 13–14, 20, 32n15, 34n20, 36n29, 55n41, 58, 111–12
Poulat, Émile, 82n12, 92n64, 112
Praet, Danny, 2, 24n70, 27–30, 32, 35–36, 40–41, 43, 46, 56, 86n28, 112
Priest, Robert D., 60n13, 112

Reinach, Salomon, 30–32, 48, 112
Renan, Ernest, 25, 49n22, 60–62, 65n28, 69n49, 70, 80n4, 82n10, 87, 88n38, 112
Rendsburg, Gary A., 8n11, 10n20, 101, 112

Resch, Richard, 92n64, 112
Reynolds, Frank E., 8n8, 113
Ricketts, Mac Linscott, 8n7, 113

Schelkens, Karim, 35–36, 113
Schepers, Judith, 28, 115
Schönborn, Christoph, 79–80n2, 80n4, 113
Schreiber, Jean-Philippe, 38, 113
Schultenover, David G., 28n2, 55, 113
Segal, Robert A., 8n7, 45n7, 113
Smith, Jonathan Z., 8n7, 113

Tacchi, Francesco, 28n2, 96
Talar, C.J.T., 6, 21, 24–25, 30, 31n12, 31n14, 32, 59n8, 62, 63n20, 82–83, 97, 113–14
Tanner, Norman P., 79n1, 114
Taylor, Charles, 50, 114
Théobald, Christoph, 24, 25n72, 60n12, 114
Thompson, Thomas L., 13, 114
Toupin-Guyot, Claire, 32–33, 114
Trémolières, François, 31–32, 114
Tsumura, David Toshio, 8n11, 114
Turvasi, Francesco, 24n69, 114

van der Wal, Ernestine, 29n7, 102
Vian, Giovanni, 1n1, 28n2, 94n6, 96

Weisberg, David B., 35n26, 95
Wernz, W. J., 24n69, 114
Wilson, R. D., 18n59, 114
Wineland, John D., 8n10, 114
Wiseman, D. J., 9n18, 10, 12, 21, 115
Wolf, Hubert, 28, 115

Yamauchi, Edwin M., 8–11, 13, 15, 19, 115–19

Zambarbieri, Annibale, 34, 119

www.ingramcontent.com/pod-product-compliance
Lightning Source LLC
Chambersburg PA
CBHW071451160426
43195CB00013B/2077